Messiah
and the
Sign of Jonah:

The Ignored Stipulation in the
Carpenter's Claim to be Messiah

Christopher Jones

Christopher Jones

Version 1.1

Also by Christopher Jones

Mashiach and the Sign of Yonah:
The Ignored Stipulation in the
Carpenter's Claim to be Mashiach
(Messianic Version)

Coming soon:

Messiah's Final 50 Days:
An Alternate Chronology in Light of
the Sign of Jonah
(Volume 2)

Messiah
and the
Sign of Jonah:

The Ignored Stipulation in the
Carpenter's Claim to be Messiah

Goal: "show me."

ACKNOWLEDGEMENTS

My sincere gratitude to everyone who supported me and contributed to this project. Of special mention:

Lois Woodman, my mother, who spent countless hours transcribing and editing the manuscript from hand-written letters while I was away on my "missionary trip."

Alex Corona, my Aztec brother and guardian deep behind enemy lines.

Luis Cardenas, my loyal friend who has stayed true through personal trials and tribulation.

Tom Feess, an ole friend whom I bounced off many of these concepts at the very earliest stage.

DEDICATION

To God Almighty
and to His only begotten Son,
who died in our stead and through whom
we are made worthy to be sons of God.
May we strive to keep His commands,
and earnestly contend for the faith
once delivered to the saints.

ambiguous?,

Table of Contents

Introduction

In the course of studying Scripture, I was struck by the fact that Jonah is the sole person with whom Jesus identifies Himself by name. Of all the Biblical characters, why Jonah – the so-called disobedient prophet? This served as the catalyst for countless hours of research and reflection. I came to understand that Jonah not only serves as the sign by which Jesus authenticates His Messianic claim, but that typology within Jonah teems with Messianic significance and ultimately asserts reconsideration of traditional Gospel chronology.

The documentation is overwhelming, but dissemination proves difficult being it imposes upon a closely guarded belief-system. There's no way of broaching the topic without invoking anger and ridicule from those who perceive it as an attack on their faith as a whole. As an example, several years ago I solicited feedback from a former pastor of mine to whom I submitted the premise of this book. Though he never refuted any of the arguments, he said the very idea was "unkind and wrong-headed." He further replied, "I imagine that you could do more harm than good for the sake of the Gospel if you try to push it."

Imagine: testing and reproving Scripture, per Paul's instruction in 2 Timothy 3:16, considered harmful; questioning doctrine and challenging tradition deemed unkind and wrong-headed!

What brand of Christianity is he peddling?! True Christianity isn't some superficial exercise in convincing the common man to make a decision for Christ; but rather it's the lifelong pursuit of righteousness, striving to grow in knowledge and grace,[1] and being transformed through the renewing of your mind.[2]

Such an obstinate perspective by shepherds-of-the-flock is classically summarized by Dave Breese in his powerful book, *Seven Men Who Rule the World From the Grave*: "Many people indeed were brought to the place where they confessed Christ, but they were brought to that place by simple preachers with a simple Gospel for the common people…there came earnest faith but not a broadly understood Christian view of God. The ranks of common people came to the point of conversion, but few were the influences of those revivals on the world of academia."[3]

Contrary to wishes of the simpleton pastor, these pages and proofs are an exercise in academia meant for the inquisitive, discerning, truth-seeking sojourner in Christ. I'm fully aware of all the deeply entrenched traditions within Christianity, and my intention is not to offend nor undermine any sacred or scholarly belief but instead to build up the Good News and to defend the faith as once delivered.

---

[1] 2 Peter 3:18

[2] Romans 12:2

[3] Breese, Dave - *Seven Men Who Rule the World From the Grave* (Chicago, IL: Moody Press, 1990) p. 154

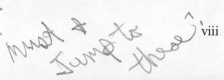

viii

With that said, I contend the historical days of the crucifixion and resurrection are not those taught from the Sunday pulpits. But how could this be -- how could millions of people reading their Bibles not have noticed something amiss? The answer, in short, is that many have; at least in terms of the numerous disparities. For example, the *Gospel of Matthew* states Mary of Magdalene witnessed the angel roll away the stone[4] while the *Gospel of Luke* states the women arrived to find the stone already rolled away.[5] These differing accounts are irreconcilable within the traditional model of Good Friday – Easter Sunday. While such seeming contradictions ought to be red-flag indications of imperfect understanding, they're instead passively dismissed as inconsequential and wholly unworthy of contention.

It's unfortunate that apathetic responses to perfectly legitimate questions have become the norm. On a broad range of issues, the Church is undisturbed in its slumber. It's as if Christians are so mind-numb from the constant barrage of information that any seemingly abstract information -- that outside of a perceived paradigm and not pertinent to salvation -- is hastily categorized as ridiculousness. Yet history bears witness this phenomenon isn't new; apathy and complacency have plagued God's people for the better part of 3500 years.

Just as problematic, people hold tradition in high esteem. Encroaching on tradition is the sentimental equivalent of trespassing on sacred ground. As a result, Christians tend to

---

[4] Matthew 28:1-2
[5] Luke 24:1-2

misconstrue any query into the matter as an attack on their faith as a whole. There's an immediate inclination to reject controversy in favor of the status quo; the Catholic Church throughout the Middle Ages being a prime, albeit dark example. Consequently, when pressed upon the numerous disparities within official dogma, Christians typically defer to the tradition's extensive history; as if duration of observance correlates to doctrinal correctness.

Ingrained since childhood -- Palm Sunday, Good Friday, and Easter Sunday are accepted givens; seemingly a paradigm never to be questioned. This preconception is so instilled in the mind's eye that all relevant information is assimilated in such a way as to never challenge the established belief. In other words, the presupposition is viewed as being so fundamental and rudimentary that even the preponderance of an alternative is outside the scope of consideration. Comfort, familiarity, and often time's sentiment towards years of yore further contribute to a subconscious blockade which harbors the paradigm. A psychological barrier obstructs the conscious mind from incorporating all of the various details with the inevitable result being orphaned information and seeming contradictions that serve to facilitate yet more confusion.

As a simplistic demonstration, indulge in the following: a man leaves home jogging. He jogs a little ways and turns left, he jogs a little ways and turns left, he jogs a little ways and turns left, and then jogs back home. As he approaches home, two masked men stand waiting for him.

<u>Questions</u>: Who are the masked men? And why did he leave home jogging?

There's nothing inherently tricky about these questions. The information is straight-forward, and the answer is sensible. Ponder the scenario again, challenge any self-imposed presumptions, and attempt to devise a hypothesis that incorporates all of the given details.

<u>Answers</u>: the masked men are the Catcher and the Umpire! The man left home jogging because he hit a home-run! It's basic sports trivia. So why are most people stumped? Because once the mind's-eye pictures *home* as being a house, the incoming information is thereafter unable to be incorporated into a viable hypothesis. Yet rather than reassessing the scenario, the mind retains its preconceived notion (house) and rejects the seemingly abstract information (masked men).

And so it is with events surrounding the crucifixion and resurrection. So ingrained are the traditional sequence of events that seemingly rogue and contradictory details are apathetically dismissed as insignificant. Yet such factoids are not Scriptural leftovers, but essential details of intentional mention by inspiration of the Holy Spirit.

> *All Scripture [is] given by inspiration of God, and [is] profitable for doctrine, for reproof, for correction, for instruction in righteousness: that the man of God may be perfect, thoroughly furnished unto all good works.*
> *(2 Timothy 3:16-17)*

With an open mind, trembling before the sacred and holy Word of the Living God, prayerfully consider the information presented herein which demonstrates the harmonization of Scripture concerning Messiah's *sign of Jonah*. While upholding the integrity of the Bible as a whole, come discover what the four Gospels truly reveal about the chronological events of that extraordinary week nearly 2,000 years ago.

> *These [Bereans] were more noble than those in Thessalonica, in that they received the word with all readiness of mind, and searched the Scriptures daily, whether those things were so. (Acts 17:11)*

Lastly, in keeping with Scriptural origins and Hebraic roots, several terms utilized throughout this book reflect an early church sentiment: *Hebrew Bible* in place of 'Old Testament,' *execution-stake*[6] in place of 'cross,' *scroll* in place of 'book,' *assembly* in place of church, and *Messiah* in place of 'Christ.'

As opposed to distractions, I intend these to disrupt familiarity with the texts just enough to aid in studying this material from a fresh perspective. May we continue to grow in the knowledge and grace of our precious Savior, Jesus Christ, and to Him be the glory both now and forever!

---

[6] The weight of historic evidence suggests Jesus was crucified upon a *Tau*-shaped timber with outstretched arms per the classical imagery. The term *execution-stake* is used herein to vividly impart its brutal reality. This is <u>not</u> advocating an upright stake with His hands secured above His head.

"He that answereth a matter
before he heareth it,
folly and shame unto him."
(Proverbs 18:13)

Chapter One

Messiah Gives a Sign

Except ye see signs and wonders,
ye will not believe. (John 4:48)

The Jonah Contention

Nothing is more captivating than the image of Jesus (*Yahshua*)[7] rising from the grave; the fact He overcame the confines of death and gloriously resurrected back to life. Jesus of Nazareth -- the Word made flesh -- bearing upon Himself the sins of the world -- dying in our stead -- laying down His life as the sacrificial Lamb of God -- and taking it up again. At one extraordinary moment in time, Jesus' cold bludgeoned corpse inhaled the breath-of-life, He opened His eyes, set aside His burial cloths, and emerged triumphant in atoning a sinful humanity to a holy Heavenly Father!

---

[7] *Yahshua* is a transliteration of the Hebrew Messiah's name. *Jesus* is neither a transliteration nor translation, as it has no meaning. According to the *Dictionary of Christian Love and Legend* by J.C.J., "It is known that the Greek name endings *sus, seus,* and *sous* were attached by the Greeks to names and geographic areas as a means to give honor to their Supreme deity, Zeus." An example is the city of *Tarsus,* from where the apostle Paul originated, meaning 'sweat of Zeus.' Consider the Spanish pronunciation of Jesus, 'Hey-Zeus.' Furthermore, *Jesus* and *Joshua* appear in Acts 7 and Hebrews 4, yet they're the identical name in Greek, *IESOUS.* Of the two, *Joshua* better approximates the Hebrew pronunciation; however, being there is no "J" sound in Hebrew, Latin, or Greek -- nor in English until the sixteenth century -- *Yahshua* is a more authentic transliteration.

1

How can one truly comprehend the magnitude of it all? It's no wonder that believers have an innate desire to venerate such an occasion; for seemingly no event in all of history is more worthy of celebration. Nevertheless, when commemorating the resurrection -- or any Biblical occasion -- it's profoundly important that unsubstantiated tradition not be mingled with direct revelation, nor fabled doctrine be construed as Scriptural truth. God's distain for heresy and paganism is manifest in His past judgments upon the children of Israel. God requires diligence in the safeguarding of truth, and ferocity in the rooting out of iniquity.

This is, by no means, skepticism directed towards His death and resurrection; for those are true and authenticated events. But similar to Israel-of-old, Christians have stumbled in their eternal vigilance. Over the past two millennia, much of Christianity has changed; little resembles the first-century churches. Long-standing traditions have evolved, new doctrines have emerged, and essential truths have been compromised. Chief among these are the alleged days of the crucifixion and resurrection, for the "official" version of events surrounding those pinnacle moments in human history is largely a work of fiction. Fallacy upon fallacy has become infused within the Gospel narratives which has corrupted the historical accounts and thereby detached believers from the full and complete knowledge of the extraordinary events which encompass Messiah's crowning achievement.

Contrary to tradition, Jesus wasn't crucified on Friday, He wasn't resurrected at sunrise, and He didn't roll aside the stone upon exiting the tomb!

These essential truths are exceptionally clear when re-examined in light of the *sign of Jonah*. Cited by Jesus on several occasions, the *sign of Jonah* is key to unlocking numerous insights lost within the corridors of antiquity. The Messianic implications inherent within Jonah are astonishing. The *Scroll of Jonah* is short -- a mere four chapters; yet in terms of Gospel chronology, Jonah changes everything!

The *Scroll of Jonah* is accepted as Scripture by Jewish, Christian, and Islamic sources. Furthermore, III Maccabees 6:8 of the *Apocrypha* records Jonah's deliverance as being one of God's great acts of mercy. The authenticity of the *Scroll of Jonah* cannot be denied, and its Messianic stipulation as invoked by the Carpenter from Nazareth must not be ignored.

Jonah and the Great Fish

To fully comprehend the *sign of Jonah*, it's necessary to first embark upon a study of the prophet himself. Jonah is the most well-known of the Minor Prophets, undoubtedly due to his notorious encounter with the great fish that swallowed him whole. Even so, while the most well-known, Jonah is the most ostracized. Three days and three nights in the belly of the great fish is viewed such an anomalous event that Jonah is the object of more skepticism than any prophet, second only to Daniel. Many scholars even question whether the *Scroll of Jonah* is a literal account or intended as purely allegorical.

The account entails Jonah being commissioned by God to warn the inhabitants of Nineveh of impending destruction as a result of their incessant evil. Jonah is reluctant about his calling and tries to flee God's presence by boarding a ship destined for the distant port of *Tarshish*. Nevertheless, God wants Jonah in Nineveh and so arranges an alternate means of transportation. While at sea, a mighty storm ensues causing Jonah to be cast overboard whereupon a great fish swallows him alive.[8] *"...And Jonah was in the belly of the great fish three days and three nights,"* after which *"...it vomited Jonah onto the dry [ground]."*[9] Jonah then obeys his commission and goes *"...to Nineveh according to the Word of the LORD."*[10]

The inhabitants of Nineveh are receptive to Jonah's message:

> So the people of Nineveh believed God, proclaimed a fast, and put on sackcloth, from the greatest to the least of them. Then word came to the king of Nineveh; and he arose from his throne and laid aside his robe, covered himself with sackcloth and sat in ashes. And he caused (it) to be proclaimed and published throughout Nineveh[.]

---

[8] Baleen whales are up to 100 feet long and 40 feet around, weighing 30,000 pounds. A Mediterranean fish recently caught and exhibited in Beirut had a head which weighed 6 tons. A man standing on the lower jaw could not reach the upper jaw... A fish caught off the Florida coast weighed 30,000 pounds. It was 45 feet long and 6 feet thick. It had a 1,500 pound fish in its stomach. It could have swallowed ten Jonahs. (*Drake Annotated Reference Bible* – Matthew 12:40)
[9] Jonah 1:17; and Jonah 2:10
[10] Jonah 3:3

4

> '[B]y decree of the king and his nobles[:] Let neither man nor beast, herd nor flock, taste anything; do not let them eat, or drink water. But let man and beast be covered with sackcloth, and cry mightily to God; yes, let everyone turn from his evil way and from the violence that is in his hands. Who can tell if God will turn and relent, and turn away from His fierce anger, so that we may not perish?'

Then God saw their works, that they turned from their evil way; and God relented from the disaster that He had said He would bring upon them, and He did not do it. (Jonah 3:5-10) — foot note?

Consequently, the city of Nineveh and its inhabitants were spared. The account serves as a powerful demonstration that God calls all people -- Hebrew and Gentile -- to repentance. Reminiscent of 2 Chronicles 7:14, the Ninevites are portrayed as humbling themselves in sackcloth and ashes, praying and fasting, seeking God's face in mercy, and turning from their wicked ways.

show this?

Yet upon witnessing their repentance, Jonah becomes angry at God and begrudgingly waits to the east of Nineveh to see whether God destroys it. Jonah erects a booth to shade himself from the scorching sun, but God prepares a gourd to rise over him in better relieving his grief. The next morning, however,

God prepares a worm to strike the gourd which immediately withers. Jonah becomes exposed to the full effects of a scorching hot sun and a powerful east wind. Jonah is so upset and miserable that he asks God to take his life.

In response to Jonah, God asks: *"And should not I spare Nineveh, that great city, wherein are more than six-score thousand persons that cannot discern between their right hand and their left hand; and* also *much cattle?"*[11] The question goes unanswered as the account abruptly terminates. There's no resolution, and no indication as to what becomes of Jonah.

Alas, the *Scroll of Jonah* is judged to be an odd account of an abstract event involving an underwhelming prophet of unsettled temperament. Hebrews came to look upon him with scorn, and Christians view him as a bad example. Jonah is seen as being a prideful, disobedient prophet with few redeeming qualities. Yet such a perspective is shallow and so far off the mark as to skew the whole of Messiah's ministry.

The Scriptural association between Jesus and Jonah is exceedingly rich. For starters, Jonah is the only Biblical character with whom Jesus associates Himself by name. Moreover, the *Scroll of Jonah* is found to incorporate four layers of meaning; reminiscent of the four Gospels which incorporate four perspectives of Messiah. The first layer within Jonah is *literal* -- Jonah's true-life happenings, the second layer is Jonah as a type of *disciple,* the third layer is Jonah as a type of *Israel,* and the fourth layer is Jonah as a type of *Messiah.*

---

[11] Jonah 4:11

When contemplating the similarities between Jesus and Jonah, most notable is the mention of *"three days and three nights";* although Catholicism and large sections of Christianity have diluted the meaning to half of its stated value. Reproving its literal context is central to this study, but the *sign of Jonah* is bigger than any of its individual components.

The *Scroll of Jonah* is laden with Messianic insight. The Christian world overlooks the Messianic implications of Jonah to its own peril. But even more compelling, the *Scroll of Jonah* proves to be the Scriptural precedent for Jesus' entire ministry, and as such it can be used to decipher and reprove many of the Messianic components within the Gospel record.

Three Days and Three nights

From healing the sick to walking on water, Jesus performed literally thousands of miracles throughout His ministry;[12] yet of those thousands, Jesus staked His claim to be Messiah upon just one. On several occasions, Jesus offered an unbelieving world a single identifying miracle -- a sole supernatural sign -- which evidences that He's the one of whom Moses and the prophets spoke; a miraculous feat that authenticates He is the Anointed of the Most High destined to lead Israel into world prominence[13] while ushering in a millennium of world peace.[14]

---

[12] John 21:25
[13] Zechariah 14:9, 16; Isaiah 2:3, 27:6; Jeremiah 3:17
[14] Revelation 20:4-6; Micah 4:3-4; Isaiah 35:1-7

It was following a heated confrontation with Pharisees who sought proof of His authority through physical displays of wonder rather than through fulfillment of Messianic prophecies when Jesus first consented to a sign. Contrary to popular opinion, the sign is not just His resurrection but entails the duration of time He would remain entombed in the heart of the earth. It's an essential distinction of extraordinary importance:

> But He [Jesus] answered and said unto them, "An evil and adulterous generation seeketh after a sign; and there shall no sign be given to it but the sign of the prophet Jonah: for as Jonah was three days and three nights in the great fish's belly; so shall the Son of Man be three days and three nights in the heart of the earth." (Matthew 12:39-40)

One authenticating attribute of the Hebrew Bible (Old Testament; referred to by Jews as the *TaNaKh*[15]) is the pre-incarnate Messiah is found on every page. For instance, Jesus is prophetically found in the people and events recorded therein which foreshadow (i.e., model, type, pre-figure) Him and events to be fulfilled in Him. In the preceding passage, Jesus indicates the prophet Jonah serves as a shadow-picture of Himself in that the *sign of Jonah* serves as the authenticating feat of His Messianic claim.

---

[15] Hebrew acronym for the Law (*Torah*), Prophets (*Nebi'im*), and Writings (*Keth b im*); equivalent to what Catholics and Christians refer to as the Old Testament.

Just as Jonah was three days and three nights in the stomach of the great fish, from which he was supernaturally delivered to save the people of Nineveh; likewise Jesus would be three days and three nights in the heart of the earth, supernaturally arising as Savior of the world!

Is it any wonder Satan instigates skepticism at the story of Jonah and the great fish in spite of it being one of the least of God's miracles?

The prophet Daniel wrote: "And he [Satan's religious hierarchy] shall speak [great] words against the most High, and shall wear out the saints of the most High, and think to change times and laws..."[16]

Given this propensity, is it not conceivable *that* the Great Deceiver would attempt to pervert knowledge of the historical days of Messiah's ministry including His crucifixion and resurrection? Is it not plausible the Serpent, that dragon of old, would cunningly endeavor to alter Jesus' duration in the heart of the earth in order to perpetuate skepticism over whether He really is who He said He is?

---

[16] Daniel 7:25, emphasis added

At last, the importance of this issue manifests: if Jesus remained three days and three nights in the heart of the earth, then in accordance with the *sign of Jonah* He miraculously demonstrated Himself to be the Messiah; however, if Jesus arose either before or after three days and three nights in the heart of the earth, then He failed to fulfill the prophetic portrait and must consequently be rejected. It's a pivotal issue of eternal magnitude -- tantamount to *is Jesus the Savior of the world, or does the world seek another*?!

Prophecy Supersedes Signs-and-Wonders

Jesus reiterated ~~the~~ that the *sign of Jonah* is to prophetically serve as a shadow-picture of Himself on at least two occasions. Their inclusion makes the *sign of Jonah* the most repeated prophecy in the Holy Bible. The *Gospel of Luke* recounts Jesus' response to one such encounter:

> *...This is an evil generation: they seek a sign; and there shall no sign be given it but the sign of Jonah the prophet. For as Jonah was a sign unto the Ninevites, so shall also the Son of Man be to this generation. (Luke 11:29-30)*

Jesus not only refused to perform on cue, but He also disparaged signs-and-wonders as a medium of authenticating His Messianic claim. He did so because signs-and-wonders are easily counterfeited by Satan and other fallen angels. For example, after Moses and Aaron cast down their rod and it

10

changed into a serpent, Pharaoh's magicians cast down their rods and theirs also changed into serpents.[17] This was not an illusion, but an authentic manifestation of the magicians' ability to tap into dark energy.[18] Pharaoh's magicians subsequently duplicated turning the Nile River into blood and inducing a plague of frogs.[19]

Understanding the superiority of prophecy over signs-and-wonders as divine authentication is crucial, for someone who is easily persuaded by signs-and-wonders will also be easily led astray by them. It happens time and again -- man's inclination towards the supernatural opens the door to deception. Messianic writings foretell:

> For there shall arise false christs and false prophets, and shall shew great signs and wonders; insomuch that, if possible, they shall deceive the very elect. (Matthew 24:24)

This tactic proves so successful in spite of Scriptural admonition that Satan will continue to engage in supernatural displays all the way through the end of the age. The apostle Paul forewarns:

> [the final anti-christ], whose coming is after the working of Satan with all power and signs and lying wonders, and with all deceivableness... (2 Thessalonians 2:9-10)

---

[17] Exodus 7:10
[18] See also Acts 16:16-18, and I Corinthians 10:19-21
[19] Exodus 7:22, 8:7

The *Scroll of Revelation* confirms this to be the end-times scenario:

> *For they are the spirits of devils, working miracles, [which] go forth unto the kings [or rulers] of the earth and of the whole world...*
> *(Revelation 16:14)*

On the other hand, fulfillment of Biblical prophecy is true authentication of the Almighty's handiwork. Jesus said, *"...that all things must be fulfilled, which were written in the [scrolls] of Moses, and the prophets, and the psalms, concerning Me."*[20] The apostle Peter affirms this when he reiterates that prophecy ranks foremost; weightier than even the apostles' personal testimonies:

> *For He [Jesus] received from God the Father honour and glory, when there came such a voice to Him from the excellent glory, 'This is My beloved Son, in whom I am well pleased.' And this voice which came from heaven we heard, when we were with Him in the holy mount. We have also a more sure word of prophecy...*
> *(2 Peter 1:17-20, emphasis added)*

In spite of being eye-witness to the healing of multitudes and conversing with Jesus in His glorified state, Peter denotes *"[over and above the apostles' personal testimonies] we have*

---

[20] Luke 24:44; see also 18:31, 24:27; John 5:39; Matthew 26:56; and Hebrews 10:7

also a more sure word of prophecy." This is because God's ability to accurately foretell world history is fundamental in distinguishing Him from charlatans. Prophecy demonstrates the LORD's[21] total transcendence of time, and He repeatedly appeals to prophecy as proof of His deity:

> *...I am God, and there is none like Me, declaring the end from the beginning and from ancient times things that are not yet done... Indeed I have spoken it; I will also bring it to pass...* (Isaiah 46:9 11)

> *Surely the LORD will do nothing, unless He [first] reveals His secret to His servants the prophets.* (Amos 3:7)

While fulfillment of Messianic prophecies most assuredly authenticate Jesus as being the Messiah to those learned in Scripture, He further offers a single miraculous sign to those unable to discern that He's the ultimate fulfillment of the Law and the Prophets; and in so doing provides a simple yea or nay validation by which to render their decision.

> *You say, 'Red sky at night, what a delight! Red sky in the morning, cloudy and storming!' You know how to read the appearance of the sky, yet you can't interpret the signs of the times? An evil and adulterous generation craves a sign, but no sign will be given to it except the sign of Jonah.* (Matthew 16:2-4, International Standard Version)

---

[21] 'LORD' in all caps denotes God's name, *YHVH*, appears in the original.

The apostle Paul critically notes, "...*the Jews require a sign, and the Greeks seek after wisdom.*"[22] So in further confounding their foolishness, Jesus offered the *sign of Jonah* as a supernatural demonstration in tantalizing their fleshly desire to be awed. Jesus then emphasized it again and again as if stressing to not be deceived by the sinister tampering of His lone authenticating performance. Why, then, do a majority of Christians reject Messiah's three days and three nights in the heart of the earth?

There are many contributing factors, but most significant is the history of Good Friday – Easter Sunday whereupon the Catholic Church, for centuries, punished any dissension from this imposed tradition by death. The ramification of such tyrannical imposition is false doctrine lingering in the twenty-first century.

The fact of the matter is that Good Friday – Easter Sunday has **not** been perpetually observed though trials and tribulation every year since the resurrection. Just the opposite, the scorn of the Church was inflicted upon all who honored the Apostolic teachings in refusing to recognize this man-made tradition that was imposed centuries after the fact by the chief of the Pagan Priesthood who's allegiance was to *Ishtar* -- the bare-breasted goddess of fertility who was allegedly re-born when she fell from heaven in a giant egg that landed in the Euphrates River whereupon she proved her divinity by turning a bird into an egg-laying rabbit.

---

[22] I Corinthians 1:22

The Deuteronomy-13 Stipulation

The Laws of God by the hand of Moses provide the Scriptural justification for challenging the Good Friday – Easter Sunday tradition. Derived from its instruction that discerning a prophet to be of God is <u>not</u> based solely upon his words coming to pass, but also upon his words being in accordance with Scripture. Found in the *Scroll of Deuteronomy,* this is important because the Almighty occasionally permits legitimate prophetic displays albeit <u>not</u> in accordance with Scripture for the purpose of testing His people's knowledge and love of Him:

> If there arise among you a prophet, or a dreamer of dreams, and giveth thee a sign or a wonder, and the sign or the wonder come to pass, whereof he spake unto thee [about] <u>other gods</u> ... thou shalt not hearken unto the[ir] words ... for the LORD your God proveth [and tests] you, to know whether ye love the LORD your God with all your heart and with all your soul. (Deuteronomy 12:32-13:3)

Therefore, knowing and studying Scripture is essential; for only fulfillment of Biblically-based prophecy constitutes reason to heed a prophet's words. This is one reason why fortune-tellers and spirit-guides among others are not to be consulted. Aside from the charlatans, the ability to tap into the spirit world is real; however, unless the source is authenticated as divine through the above methodology, let the hearer beware!

15

Don't be fooled into believing the Deuteronomy-13 stipulation is relegated to a former Covenant. John the Revelator confirms this to be fully applicable in the New Covenant:

[/as to]

> Beloved/ believe not every spirit, but try the spirits whether they are of God: because many false prophets are gone out into the world. (1 John 4:1)

have

Naturally, when Jesus consented to an authenticating sign, He subjugated Himself to this same standard: 1) His sign of three days and three nights in the heart of the earth must come to pass, and 2) His sign must have Scriptural precedent; otherwise He must <u>not</u> be hearkened to, but put to death.[23]

There's not a lot of wiggle room. Jesus' explicit adherence to Deuteronomy-13 is mandated. The latter stipulation of Scriptural precedence is found in the prophet Jonah; i.e., the reason Jesus refers to it as the *sign of Jonah*. Consequently, the sole component in need of validation is that He remained in the heart of the earth for *"three days and three nights"* in like manner as the prophet Jonah.

Clearly, because so much hinges upon whether Jesus is who He says He is, it's not a trivial matter. At stake is a question of eternal significance: could Jesus be a false prophet whom the Almighty allowed to foretell His own death and resurrection -- although which came to pass contrary to how He foretold -- as a test to see who rejects His counterfeit claim per Biblical

---

[23] Deuteronomy 13:5

16

mandate? Could Jesus be a false Messiah allowed to go forth into the world to determine who is learned enough to reject authentic signs and wonders which lack Scriptural precedent? Could the Almighty have permitted Jesus to impersonate the Messiah -- with the true Messiah, as the Jews believe, still to come -- for the purpose of requiring His people to prove their love through rejecting the Carpenter from Nazareth?

It's an earth-shaking concept, yet a decision Deuteronomy-13 stipulates be made. The inevitable conclusion of the Good Friday – Easter Sunday tradition is that Jesus, at most, was dead and buried three days and two nights. It's a disparity with eternal consequences, and ought to pierce every Christian to their soul. Good Friday – Easter Sunday insinuates Jesus was an imposter; a false Messiah who spawned a false religion and in so doing condemned billions of people to hell amid the greatest deception of all time!

It's a sobering realization, but take comfort in knowing Jesus is the true Messiah, and in the knowledge that He did fulfill the *sign of Jonah*. Scripture is emphatic on these points. Yet there's clearly a fundamental problem with Good Friday – Easter Sunday; an irreconcilable problem being it's not scripturally sound doctrine. Per the *sign of Jonah* and the stipulation of Deuteronomy-13, Jesus could not have been crucified on Friday and resurrected on Sunday.

Chapter Two

Interpreting Messiah's Sign

For if ye believe not that I am He,
ye shall die in your sins. (John 8:24)

In Messiah's Own Words

In recognition of the fact He'd shed His blood on behalf of humanity, Jesus frequently spoke about His impending execution as well as the duration of time He would remain entombed. Jesus clearly considered them important aspects for His disciples to grasp, even if after the fact. Yet the importance of His duration in the heart in the earth has been lost down through the centuries. Today most people believe Jesus merely said, *"... [on] the third day He shall rise again,"*[24] making it easy to accept the view He meant only partial days. However, besides Jesus' statements to rise *"on the third day"* and to remain *"in the heart of the earth for three days and three nights,"* there are additional statements to be taken into consideration.

On one occasion Jesus declared, *"Destroy this Temple and in three days I will raise it up."*[25] On another occasion Jesus foretold *"...the Son of Man must suffer many things, and be*

---

[24] Luke 18:33; see also 9:22, 24:7, 24:46; Matthew 16:21, 17:23, 20:19; Acts 10:40; and 1 Corinthians 15:4

[25] John 2:19, emphasis added; see also Mark 14:58

rejected of the elders, and [of] the chief priests and scribes, and be killed, and <u>after</u> three days rise again."[26] In fact, following His entombment, as the Pharisees pled with the Roman *Prefect of Judaea*[27] (governor) to post guards at the tomb as assurance His disciples didn't steal the corpse, they recounted this very quote: "… *Sir, we remember that that deceiver said, while He was yet alive, '<u>After</u> three days I will rise again.'*"[28]

Consider the totality of Jesus' statements: *"after three days"* refers to a period of time 72-hours or further into the future; *"on the third day"* refers to a period of time 48- to 72 hours into the future; and *"in three days"* refers to a period of time not more than 72-hours. Hence, the sole common denominator in every instance is 72-hours. In other words, *"three days and three nights;"* which is precisely as Jesus articulated to the Pharisees when offering the *sign of Jonah*.

Moreover, the ongoing theme of three days prevails throughout Scripture. From the prevalence of three days in the prophecies of Joseph,[29] to Moses causing three days of darkness in the land of Egypt;[30] from a twelve-year-old Jesus being discovered in the Temple after missing for three days,[31] to the apostle Paul, while on the road to Damascus, being blinded for three days.[32] This re-occurring prophetic pattern

---

[26] Mark 8:31, emphasis added

[27] Herry Vardaman, *A New Inscription Which Mentions Pilate as "Prefect,"* Journal of Biblical Literature 81 (1962) 70–71.

[28] Matthew 27:63, emphasis added

[29] Genesis 40:12-23

[30] Exodus 10:22-23

[31] Luke 2:43-46

[32] Acts 9:7-9

appears a total of 75 times throughout the Holy Bible; 62 times preceding the New Covenant.

Is it possible the three days of darkness that consumed Egypt was in reality 36-hours? Is it possible the three days when the adolescent Jesus was missing was merely a day and one-half? Is it possible the three days Paul was rendered blind was in actuality half of the implied duration? Clearly, to suggest Jesus was buried Friday evening and resurrected Sunday morning is to likewise challenge the integrity of God's Word from the *Scroll of Genesis* through the *Acts of the Apostles*.

Six Days from Jericho

As fate would have it, failing to allow the necessary time to fulfill the *sign of Jonah* is not the sole impediment to a Friday crucifixion. There are numerous contradictions as well as a Sabbath transgression; namely, Jesus' journey from Jericho to Bethany. John 12:1 specifies, *"Then Jesus six days before [His crucifixion on] the Passover came to Bethany [from Jericho[33]]."* If Passover occurred on Friday, then six days prior would be Saturday -- the weekly Sabbath. This is problematic in that Jesus would not have spent the Sabbath day traveling. Although Jesus didn't pay homage to rabbinic law [*takanot*][34] limiting a Sabbath's day journey to 2000 cubits (.9 kilometers) beyond the city wall -- in fact, such are the burdensome yokes

[33] Luke 19:1, 28
[34] Laws within Judaism that carry the same weight, and in some cases supersede, the authority and commands of Scripture.

that Jesus railed against -- assuredly He honored and obeyed the Sabbath command:

> *See! For the LORD has given you the Sabbath;*
> *therefore He gives you on the sixth day bread for*
> *two days. Let every man remain in his place; let*
> *no man go out of his place on the seventh day.*
> *(Exodus 16:29)*

In theorizing Jesus violated the Scriptural command by spending the better part of the Sabbath traveling, Jesus is essentially crowned the hypocrite of hypocrites. After all, this is the Man who forewarned, *"And pray that your flight may not be in winter or on the Sabbath."*[35]

Nevertheless, the contention is without merit per New Covenant writings which record Jesus continually in the synagogues teaching and healing on the Sabbath;[36] never traveling. Furthermore, there's no Pharisaic accusation of Jesus violating the Sabbath when traveling to Bethany.

In delving into His prophetic role as the Passover Lamb, Jesus had to be without spot or blemish (i.e., without sin; without having transgressed the Law).[37] In order for Jesus to be without sin, He couldn't be in violation of the Scriptural command to remain in His place on the Sabbath. With Jesus obediently remaining in His place on the Sabbath, He couldn't have

---

[35] Matthew 24:20
[36] Luke 4:14-15, 16, 31, 44
[37] 2 Corinthians 5:21

traveled from Jericho to Bethany on Saturday. Being Jesus didn't travel from Jericho to Bethany on Saturday, His crucifixion six days later couldn't have been on Friday.

A Friday crucifixion is a preposterous assertion argued from a position of Scriptural ignorance; for if Messiah's crucifixion occurred on Friday, then He broke the fourth commandment and was a transgressor totally incapable of atoning for the sins of mankind in the first place. On the other hand, knowing Jesus is neither a liar, a hypocrite, nor a Sabbath-breaker, Friday is the one day which can be definitively eliminated from being the day of Messiah's crucifixion.

Arguments for Partial Days

The history of Good Friday – Easter Sunday and its induction into the Church is an enlightening study, but far too lengthy to be covered here (see *Appendix: A Brief History of Church Persecution*). Yet the tradition is largely sustained through two Scriptural references: Mark 15:42, which records the day following the crucifixion as being a Sabbath; and Luke 24:1, which records the women's arrival at the tomb at sunrise on Sunday. When the crucifixion – resurrection scenario is built *upon* these verses rather than in agreement *with* these verses, it can appear Jesus was buried late Friday and arisen early Sunday. However, if Good Friday – Easter Sunday is factual, then Jesus failed; for it's impossible to account for three days and three nights in between Friday evening and Sunday morning.

Nevertheless, instead of disavowing this tradition as completely incompatible with the *sign of Jonah*, men are prone to invent theological reasons as to why Messiah's sign isn't to be taken at face value.

In a vain attempt to rationalize Jesus being dead and buried for only half of the avowed time, some scholars argue that in Greek *"three days and three nights"* can refer to three periods consisting either of day or night. Thus, Jesus being placed in the tomb at sunset on Friday and arising at sunrise on Sunday fulfills three such periods: one day and two nights.

The fact of the matter is the Hebraic mindset is completely foreign to such rationale. Jesus was incarnated as a Hebrew man, born of a Hebrew virgin, and raised in a Hebrew culture. His disciples were Hebrew, He verbally sparred with Pharisees in Hebrew, and He referenced the Hebrew *Scroll of Jonah* wherein *"three days and three nights"* inarguably denotes a literal 72-hours. To theorize Jesus invoked the sign of a Hebrew prophet before a Hebrew audience with a Hebraic mindset as proof He's the Hebrew Messiah, and then fulfilled that sign through a Grecian reckoning of periods defies all logic.

Further substantiating this Hebraic perspective and a literal interpretation is the *Scriptural Law of First Mention* wherein the Creator's definition of 'three days and three nights' is plainly defined within the onset of Genesis:

> ...*God divided the light from the darkness. And God called the light 'Day,' and the darkness He*

called 'Night.' And the evening and the morning were the first day... And the evening and the morning were the second day... And the evening and the morning were the third day.
(Genesis 1:4-13)

Clearly, Scriptural precedent as cited in the Genesis account of creation advocates three literal periods of darkness and three literal periods of light.

Taking this into account, others contend the darkness that covered the land from the sixth hour through the ninth hour while Jesus hung on the execution-stake[38] fulfilled one of the three periods of darkness. Thus, Friday morning is the first period of light, Friday afternoon (12- to 3 PM) the first period of dark, Friday evening the second period of light, Friday night the second period of dark, Saturday the third period of light, and Saturday night the third period of dark.

It's a clever theory, but replete with problems. For instance, in overcoming the fact Jesus wasn't dead amid the first periods of light and dark, it's claimed Jesus was *as good as dead* upon His condemnation. Additionally, in fulfilling the requirement that He actually be *"in the heart of the earth"* during those periods, it's claimed from the moment Jesus was condemned that He *experienced* hell.

---

[38] Mark 15:33; Luke 23:44-45; Matthew 27:45

It's a colorful interpretation, but only serves to demonstrate the borderless realm of human rationalization by which mankind justifies disregarding the Almighty's instructions.

Three Day Idiomatic Expression

Far and away the most common contention is that Jesus implemented an idiomatic expression incorporating portions of three days. This is based upon a pretext of Hebrew culture wherein any portion of a day can be reckoned as a whole day. Circumcision, for example, occurs on the eighth day regardless of when on the first day a child is born.[39] *The Jewish Encyclopedia* elaborates: "...circumcision takes place on the eighth day, even though, of the first day only a few minutes after the birth of the child, these being counted as one [full] day."[40]

In this sense it's true -- the eighth day is calculated regardless of when on the first day the clock starts. However, circumcision on the eighth day is entirely different than circumcision upon the completion of eight days and eight nights. When both days and nights are invoked, it unequivocally ceases to be an idiomatic expression. 'Day and night' always denotes a full 24-hour period and does not infer any portion thereof; nor does *"three days and three nights"* infer portions of three 24-hour periods. In like fashion, when both 'evening and

---

[39] Genesis 17:12; see also Luke 1:59 and 2:21
[40] *Jewish Encyclopedia,* Vol. 4, p. 475

morning' are invoked, it denotes a full 24-hour period.[41] Hence, the day/night and evening/morning methodology always infers a full 24-hour day, and it serves as the death knell to Jesus' sign being reckoned as an idiomatic expression.

Aside from the *Scroll of Jonah*, there are two other mentions of 'three days and three nights' in the Hebrew Bible (Old Testament). The first occurs in the *Scroll of Samuel*:

> *And they found an Egyptian in the field, and brought him to [King] David, and gave him bread, and he did eat; and they made him drink water; and they gave him a piece of a cake of figs, and two clusters of raisins: and when he had eaten, his spirit came again to him: for he had eaten no bread, nor drunk any water, three days and three nights.*
> *(1 Samuel 30:11-12, emphasis added)*

There's nothing particularly insightful about this account other than its mention of 'days and nights' which categorically excludes it from being an idiomatic expression. It clearly denotes a period approximating 72-hours (as opposed to as little as 25-hours), and is corroborated by the fact the Egyptian wasn't merely hungry and thirsty, but semi-conscious and on the verge of death.

---

[41] Gen 1:5, 8, 13, 19, 23, 31; Ex 16:8, 12, 13; 18:13-14, 27:21, 29:39, 41; Lev 24:3; Num 9:15, 21; 28:4; Deut 28:67; 1 Kings 17:16; 2 Kings 16:15; 1 Chron 16:40, 23:30; 2 Chron 2:4, 13:11, 31:3; Ezra 3:3; Job 4:20; Psalms 55:17, 65:8, 90:6; Ecc 11:16; Daniel 8:14, 26.

On the other hand, 'three days and three nights' within the *Scroll of Esther* is a bit more of a case study. Haman, the villain in the account, devised a plan to eradicate the Hebrews from the Persian Empire that encompassed 127 kingdoms spanning from Ethiopia to India. As Queen Esther prepared to approach King Ahasuerus[42] in the inner-court about the matter without summons, an act for which she'd be killed lest the king extended his golden scepter, she plead for her fellow Hebrews to join her -- and her maidens -- in a 72-hour fast to the Almighty:

> Go, gather together all the [Hebrews] that are present in [the city of] Shushan, and fast ye for me, and neither eat nor drink <u>three days, night or day</u>: I also and my maidens will fast likewise; and so will I go in unto the king, which [is] not according to the law: and if I perish, I perish.
> (Esther 4:16, emphasis added)

Per Esther's request, the Hebrews all refrained from eating and drinking for "*three days, night or day.*" Scripture reckons days sunset to sunset,[43] so 'night and day' equates to the natural progression through one day. The Hebrews all understood this. Therefore, in the course of appealing to the Almighty for deliverance, they prayed and fasted from the start of the first day (sunset) through the completion of the third day (sunset); "*three days, night [and] day*" being a full 72-hours.

---

[42] *King Ahasuerus* is also known by the Greek rendering of *Xerxes*, who ruled Persia from 486-465 BCE

[43] Genesis 1:4-31; Leviticus 23:32

Meanwhile, on the third day, Esther entered the inner-court of King Ahasuerus to invite him to a banquet later that evening:

> *Now it came to pass on the third day that Esther put on her royal apparel, and stood in the inner-court of the king's house, over against the king's house: and the king sat upon his royal throne in the royal house, over against the gate of the house. (Esther 5:1)*

Esther approaching the king *"on the third day"* doesn't negate the ongoing fast. Quite to the contrary, Esther was in the midst of their third day of fasting when she risked her life going before the king without summons. There's no inference the fast, at this point, was over; in fact, how absurd to contemplate the Hebrews had terminated their fast at the hour when in most need of divine favor.

Conversely, on the third day of the ongoing fast, Esther indeed found favor in the king's sight as he extended his golden scepter and accepted the invitation for him and Haman to attend her banquet later that evening. Then, as the Hebrews continued to fast for divine intervention through sunset, it was during the evening banquet when completion of the 72-hours came to pass.

Thereafter, favor was again found as King Ahasuerus accepted Esther's invitation for him and Haman to attend a subsequent banquet the following evening. It was at the second banquet, 24-hours after the completion of the 72-hour fast, wherein

Haman's sinister plot was foiled and the Hebrews' deliverance was manifest.

Third Day of the Week

In examining all aspects of *"the third day,"* the terminology may also designate the day of the week, i.e. the modern equivalent of *Tuesday*. Scripture doesn't record days of the week according to the pagan devised names that are commonplace today. Corresponding to the seven "wandering" celestial bodies, modern days of the week are named in honor of ancient pagan deities: Sun's Day – *Sol Invictus Mithras* (day of the unconquerable sun, Mithras); Moon's Day – identified with *Artemis* (Diana); Tiu's Day (Mars) – Norse deity of war; Woden's Day (Mercury) – Celtic deity skilled in magic; Thor's Day (Jupiter) – Celtic deity of thunder; Frigga's Day (Venus) – fertility goddess, wife of Woden and mother of Tiu and Thor; and Seterne's day (Saturn) – Roman deity of agriculture.

The following excerpt from Justin Martyr, a second-century Christian apologist, exemplifies this pagan origin of days' names when writing of the risen Savior: "...and on the day after that of Saturn, which is the day of the Sun, having appeared to His apostles and disciples, He taught them..."[44]

Biblically-speaking, days of the week are effectively referred to by their place-number: *the first day, the second day, the*

---

[44] *First Apology of Justin*, Chapter LXVII - Weekly Worship of the Christians

third day, the fourth day, the fifth day, the sixth day, and
the Sabbath.

Biblical Reckoning vs. Pagan Reckoning

	Night	Day	Night	Day	Night	Day	Night	Day	Night	Day	Night	Day	Night	Day
Biblical Days:	1st		2nd		3rd		4th		5th		6th		Sabbath	
Pagan Days:	Sun		Moon		Tiu's		Woden's		Thor's		Frigga's		Saturn	

A textbook example is found in the account of John the
Revelator wherein a wedding occurs on *the third day*:

> *The day following, Jesus would go forth into
> Galilee... And <u>the third day</u> there was a marriage
> in Cana of Galilee; and the mother of Jesus was
> there. (John 1:43, 2:1, emphasis added)*

This doesn't indicate Jesus and His disciples departed
Jerusalem[45] and traveled at an exhausting pace in order to
arrive in Cana on the second day and then attend this wedding
the third day later. Rather, the implication is they departed
Jerusalem and went to Galilee as Jesus directed, then in the
coming days Jesus and His disciples were invited[46] and
summarily attended the said wedding on *the third day* of the
week.

---

[45] John 1:43
[46] John 2:2

Hebrews don't marry on *the Sabbath* because the Almighty blessed and sanctified it as a day of rest in commemoration of creation.[47] They may, however, marry on any other day of the week. Weddings on *the third day* became popular with the rationale it's the day God twice saw His creation was good, and therefore is considered a day of double blessing.

> *And God said, 'Let the waters under the heaven be gathered together unto one place, and let the dry [ground] appear': and it was so. And God called the dry [ground] 'Earth;' and the gathering together of the waters He called 'Seas:' and <u>God saw that [it was] good</u>. And God said, 'Let the earth bring forth grass, the herb yielding seed, [and] the fruit tree yielding fruit after its kind, whose seed [is] in itself, upon the earth:' and it was so. And the earth brought forth grass, herb yielding seed after his kind, and the tree yielding fruit, whose seed [is] in itself, after its kind: <u>and God saw that [it was] good</u>. And the evening and the morning were the third day. (Genesis 1:9-13, emphasis added)*

So it's fitting *the third day,* the day of double blessing, was a favored day to exchange vows and enter into a new covenant as a blessed union of husband and wife.

Ironically, Christian tradition is the complete opposite with couples customarily marrying on no other day but *the Sabbath*.

---

[47] Genesis 2:2

Returning to the matter at hand, there's no contention Jesus was raised on *the third day* in this sense, as Tuesday is clearly not the day of Messiah's resurrection.

Similarly, *the third day* may also designate the day of the month as it does in 1 Samuel 20:5, but there's likewise no contention Jesus was raised on *the third day* in that sense. When in context of Messiah's resurrection, *the third day* always denotes the passing of a full three days time.

Literal Interpretation

Although an element of context and style is always lost in translation, further diluting the text's full impact is the evolution of language over time. Nevertheless, dialogue in millennia past wasn't as primitive as one might presume. The languages of the Bible, specifically Hebrew and Greek, are highly developed communication systems; and in certain respects more so than English.

Of particular interest are words in both Hebrew and Greek that denote an incomplete unit. Found in Daniel 7:25 and Revelation 12:14, they designate the 'dividing of time'; rendered *'half a time'* in the phrase *"time, times, and half a time."*[48] The implication is that if Jesus had been entombed for portions of days, then Scripture would be apt to use this literary devise to convey so; i.e. 'the dividing of day (Friday),

---

[48] See also Daniel 12:7

day (Saturday), and the dividing of day (Sunday).' Scripture's failure to implement a 'dividing of time' specification into the three days of Jesus' entombment is further affirmation of their literal context.

Along these same lines, in contemplating Jesus' hurried burial in the closing moments of the day following His crucifixion, tabulating those few remaining minutes after the stone was rolled in front of the tomb -- presuming any at all -- as one of three days is highly disingenuous. It's the modern equivalent of issuing a three day ultimatum at 11 PM, and then demanding a response shortly after 12 AM on the following night. It's technically the third day, but the qualifier is misleading and designed to deceive. Such attributes are the exact opposite of the Man of whom the volume of Scripture is written.[49]

Moreover, Jesus personally sustained the definition of 'day' as set forth in the Genesis account as consisting of evening (dark) and morning (light), and in so doing stipulates both *night* and *day* each constitute half of the literal 24-hour period:

> *Jesus answered, 'Are there not <u>twelve hours in the day</u>? If any man walk in the day, he stumbleth not, because he seeth the light of this world. But if a man walk in the night, he stumbleth, because there is no light in him. (John 11:9-10, emphasis added)*

---

[49] Psalms 40:7, Hebrews 10:7

To add context to His statement, an hour in ancient times wasn't measured according to the atomic clock as its reckoned today, but rather it comprised one twelfth of either the lighted or darkness portion of each day. An hour of daylight consisted of one twelfth of the time from sunrise to sunset regardless of season or latitude. Therefore, a day-hour was longer in the summer and shorter in the winter, and a night-hour vice versa. Ancient texts often refer to this method of reckoning as a "Talmudic hour."

Basically it means that even though they lasted for different durations,[50] both *day* and *night* each consisted of twelve hours, and that Jesus confirmed this to be applicable within a Biblical context.

Night/dark (12-hours) and day/light (12-hours) equates to 24-hours. Three days (36-hours) and three nights (36-hours) equates to 72-hours. To rationalize otherwise is to reject the simplicity of Scripture and to reject the authority of both testaments.

Lastly, a final instance of literal context is found in the *Scroll of Revelation* wherein two end-times witnesses lay dead in the streets of Jerusalem for three and one-half days before being raised back to life:

> *And they of the people and kindreds and*
> *tongues and nations shall see their dead bodies*

---

[50] Early on, night was divided into three or four *watches,* but later it came to be reckoned as twelve hours in like manner as its daylight counterpart.

> *three days and an half,* and shall not suffer their
> dead bodies to be put in graves ... And *after*
> *three days and an half* the Spirit of life from God
> entered into them, and they stood upon their
> feet; and great fear fell upon them which saw
> them. (Revelation 11:9-11; emphasis added)

If reference to 'days' truly applied to any portion thereof, then reference to 'half a day' would make no sense. What is 'half of any portion of a day'? Furthermore, why does Scripture here specify *"after three days and an half"* as opposed to simply *"on the fourth day"* when this event could supposedly come to pass at any moment on the fourth day?

The answer, of course, is that it's meant to be applied literally. For those privileged enough to watch this event unfold in the not too distant future, expect the two witnesses to arise midway through the fourth day; 84-hours after their martyrdom. Likewise, in the case of Jesus, *"three days and three nights"* is to be applied literally; with Messiah arising 72-hours after being enclosed *"in the heart of the earth."*

Seriously folks, if it weren't a necessity to manipulate, shape, and fashion Scripture to accommodate the antiquated Good Friday – Easter Sunday tradition, then none of this partial day, figure-of-speech, Grecian reckoning, darkness that covered the land, allegorical fulfillment, as-good-as-dead ridiculousness would carry any merit at all.

When it comes to clarifying the sole miraculous sign through which all humanity shall be held accountable to acknowledge Jesus as Messiah, the Almighty doesn't offer some vaguely defined or trick interpretation by which to deceive as many people as possible. That's Satan's task.

God relays the account of Jonah as a pretext, and then spells it out plainly: *"For as Jonah was three days and three nights in the great fish's belly; so shall the Son of Man be three days and three nights in the heart of the earth."*[51] God reaffirms the *sign of Jonah* by making it the most repeated prophecy in all of Scripture, and then emphasizes it over and over through types and shadow-pictures (see: Chapter Five).

Most people are persuaded by the Scriptural argument for a literal three days and three nights, but tradition and their churches tell them otherwise. Furthermore, because of confusion instigated by the Good Friday – Easter Sunday tradition, questions linger as to when the events of Passion Week actually came to pass. Most notably, upon what day of the week was Jesus crucified -- was it Wednesday? Or was it Thursday? It has to be one or the other, because it certainly wasn't Friday!

---

[51] Matthew 12:40

Chapter Three
Hour of Burial & Resurrection

Let us hear the conclusion of the whole matter:
Fear God and keep His commandments;
for this is the whole duty of man (Ecclesiastes 12:13)

Time of Messiah's Burial

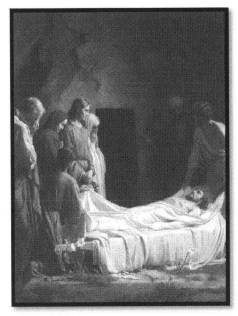

According to the Law of God by the hand of Moses, dead bodies are to be buried the same day in which someone dies.[52] Since days are reckoned from evening to evening, burial must occur prior to nightfall on the same day death occurs.

In examining the accounts of Jesus' crucifixion, the Gospels record He died shortly after the ninth hour; equivalent to three o'clock in the afternoon.[53] Yet irrespective of His death, His body remained

---

[52]Deuteronomy 21:22-23
[53] Luke 23:44-46; see also Matthew 27:45-50 and Mark 15:33.

affixed to the execution-stake until the sun began to set. It's then when Joseph of Arimathea, having secured custody of the corpse from Pontius Pilate, finally detached Jesus from the timber and readied Him for a quick burial.[54]

Nicodemus, a Pharisee who believed Jesus to be the Messiah, brought a mixture of myrrh and aloes, and assisted Joseph with wrapping the corpse in linen cloths.[55] Late in the day, they hurriedly carried Him to a nearby tomb, laid Him inside, and Joseph rolled the stone door shut.[56] With the Sabbath imminent,[57] the two men immediately departed.[58]

Although impossible to derive the exact minute at which Jesus was enclosed within the tomb, for all intents and purposes *evening* marks that moment in time. Evening, or twilight, is the starting point of the three days and three nights wherein Jesus remained in the heart of the earth.

Time of Messiah's Resurrection

Biblically speaking, one day doesn't immediately roll over into the next as it does with a midnight reckoning. Rather, the buffer between days consists of a period of time known as *evening*. It's synonymous with *twilight*, and consists of that

---

[54] Matthew 27:57-58; see also Mark 15:43-46 and Luke 23:50-53
[55] John 19:39-40
[56] Matthew 27:59-60
[57] John 19:42
[58] Matthew 27:60; see also Mark 15:46.

short span of illumination between when the sun has set and when it becomes fully dark. Its duration varies depending upon latitude and atmospheric conditions, but twilight essentially lasts half-an-hour.

The term *evening* is derived from the Hebrew word ערב or `*ereb* (Strong's H6153), meaning 'mixed' and 'mingled'. By definition, *evening* correlates to the time when two days mingle together. The Gospels convey this is exactly when Joseph of Arimathea rolled the large stone over the tomb's entrance and enclosed Jesus within the heart of the earth. Luke describes that moment in time as *"the [end of] Preparation Day, and the Sabbath was just beginning."*[59]

Evening, or twilight, is an easy reference point from which to calculate three days and three nights; no need to consider partial days. Jesus, after fulfilling three days and three nights in the heart of the earth, likewise arose at twilight; upon the full and literal completion of the third day!

Then, when the women arrived Sunday morning, they found the large stone enclosing the tomb to be already rolled aside. An angel proclaimed, *"Why seek ye the living among the dead? He is not here, but is risen..."*[60] This is because Jesus had arisen the previous evening; on what God deems the completion of *the Sabbath*, but on what the world reckons as Saturday.

---

[59] Luke 23:54, *International Standard Version*
[60] Luke 24:5-6

41

Mary's Arrival at the Tomb

Further verification that Jesus arose Saturday evening is found in scrutinizing the accounts of the women arriving at the tomb; in particular that there were multiple occurrences. The best known account is the *Gospel of Luke* wherein the women arrive at the tomb at sunrise on Sunday, but the *Gospel of John* records an entirely different event:

> The first [day] of the week cometh Mary [of] Magdalene early, <u>when it was yet dark</u>, unto the sepulcher... (John 20:1, emphasis added)

This conveys that Mary of Magdalene, along with Mary the mother of James per Matthew 28:1, ventured to the tomb Saturday evening immediately after the Sabbath ended; by God's reckoning, amid the mingling of Saturday and Sunday.

The Gospel of John doesn't specify this. All it indicates is that it was dark; i.e. approximately 6 PM to 5 AM.[61] Yet with this information, much can be construed. First, with the two Marys so anxious as to set out into the darkness, there's no rationale in their delaying until the pre-dawn hours as opposed to as soon as the sun had set. Second, it's absurd to contemplate the two Marys scurrying alone through the streets at 4- to 4:30 AM. It's more sensible that with the sun having set about 6:00 PM, the two Marys immediately ventured out into the darkness of a new day. Therein the two Marys walked openly

---

[61] Springtime in Israel; no Daylight Savings Time

and safely through the city streets as the inhabitants began to emerge from their Sabbath rest.

The terminology "... *when it was yet dark*" can relay the false impression it had been dark for an extended period of time, and therein appear to substantiate the pre-dawn perspective. However, the word translated *yet* is derived from the Greek word ἔτι or *eti* (Strong's #G2089), the primary definition being: 'of a thing which went on formerly, whereas now a different state of things exists or has begun to exist.'

In context, the two Marys arriving at the tomb in darkness constitutes the former state of existence (John 20:1-2) whereas the subsequent events after sunrise constitute the newer state of existence (John 20:3-23). Hence, ἔτι is an adverb reinforcing the fact it was dark (6 PM to 5 AM) when the two Marys arrived at Jesus' tomb; not an indicator as to the duration of that darkness.

Complicit with the two Marys arriving in a state of darkness is the realization the Gospel accounts do not uniformly document the same event, nor are the numerous discrepancies within the Gospels merely insignificant variations within the recollections of the authors. To the contrary, the texts illustrate separate and distinct occurrences of women arriving at the tomb: one angel versus two angels, an encounter inside the tomb versus an encounter outside the tomb, guards versus no guards, earthquake versus no earthquake, and sunlight versus darkness.

Additionally, the Gospels specify that Mary of Magdalene witnessed the angel roll away the stone[62] while the women Sunday morning found the stone already rolled away,[63] and that Mary of Magdalene encountered the risen Savior[64] while the other women encountered angels declaring He's risen.[65] The Gospel record explicitly depicts Mary of Magdalene arriving at the tomb apart from the other women, and she did so Saturday evening upon Jesus' completion of *"three days and three nights in the heart of the earth."*

Please note Jesus did not roll aside the large stone when He departed the tomb. When the two Marys arrived, there was an earthquake followed by an angel from heaven who came and rolled aside the stone in revealing the tomb is empty!

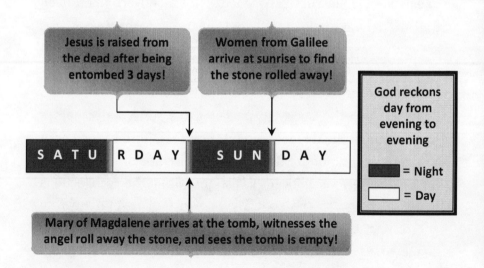

---

[62] Matthew 28:2
[63] Mark 16-2-4; Luke 24:1-2
[64] Matthew 28:9-10
[65] Mark 16:5-9; Luke 24:4-8

Two Earthquakes in Matthew

Accentuating Jesus' death and resurrection is the pair of earthquakes recorded in the *Gospel of Matthew*. Several fault-lines run near Jerusalem, so earthquakes aren't an unexpected phenomenon; in fact, half a dozen major quakes have rocked the city over the past millennia.[66] Nevertheless, there's a distinction between an *earthquake* caused by seismic activity and the *trembling of the earth*[67] caused by the presence of God.

When His holiness is manifest upon earth, the elements stir and creation trembles. This is evident in the relaying of the *Oracles of God* upon Mount Sinai, and it will continue to be the case through Messiah's Second Coming as foretold in the *Scroll of Revelation*.

The first of the two notable quakes occurred on the day of His crucifixion at three o'clock in the afternoon when Jesus bowed His head and gave up the ghost.[68] The spiritual ramifications of this quake included the six-foot thick veil inside the Temple which separated the Holy Place from the Holy of Holies being torn in two, and the saints-of-old awakening in their graves.[69]

---

[66] http://www.nbcnews.com/id/3980139/ns/technology_and_science-science/t/jerusalems-old-city-risk-earthquake/

[67] Judges 5:4; 2 Sam 22:8 ; Psalms 77:18, 97:4, and 104:32

[68] Matthew 27:46-50, Mark 15:34-37, John 19:30

[69] Matthew 27:52

The second quake occurred Saturday evening when the two Marys arrived at His tomb, and immediately preceded the angel rolling aside the large stone.[70] The spiritual ramifications of this quake entailed the graves of the saints-of-old being opened, and the saints arising and going forth into Jerusalem.[71] This is indication that the quake was more than mere dramatics in anticipation of the angel coming down and revealing the tomb to be empty; it was the actual moment of Jesus' resurrection, i.e. His holy presence being manifest inside the still enclosed tomb!

After *"three days and three nights in the heart of the earth,"* Jesus took up His life again, set aside His burial cloths, and departed through the stone surroundings in like manner as He would enter the upper-room via passing through walls.[72] Immediately after His departure, an angel came down from heaven to roll aside the large stone in showcasing to the two Marys the grand implication of what had just transpired in the tomb in front of them.

While nobody saw Jesus' corpse inhale the breath-of-life and arise, to say there were no witnesses to the resurrection isn't entirely true. The two Marys were there! The two Marys felt the earth tremble when Jesus' spirit returned to Him! And the two Marys saw the angel descend from heaven and roll aside the stone in revealing Jesus to be risen and gone!

---

[70] Matthew 28:2
[71] Matthew 27:53
[72] John 20:19, Luke 24:36

Yet this revelation is lost amid the Good Friday – Easter Sunday tradition wherein everything is amalgamated into a singular Sunday morning event. And so it must be, because when Messiah's crucifixion is alleged to have occurred on Friday, there can be no witnesses to His resurrection on Saturday!

Misplaced Comma in Mark 16:9

People are naturally skeptical upon first hearing Jesus wasn't resurrected at Sunday sunrise; after all, it's usually a teaching ingrained since one's spiritual infancy. Nevertheless, not a single verse of Scripture specifies the resurrection to have occurred early Sunday morning. Mark 16:9 may appear to be the exception, but its implication of an early morning resurrection is derived from a translational flaw. It's typically translated as follows:

> Now when Jesus was risen early the first [day] of the week, He appeared first to Mary [of] Magdalene, out of whom He had cast seven devils.

All English versions of the New Covenant are translated from Greek, a language that doesn't utilize commas. Therefore, in English, a comma can be added or deleted or moved, and it doesn't technically alter Scripture; though it may distort its meaning. Commas were added for the purpose of improving clarity; however, occasionally commas and other punctuation were incorrectly inserted as a result of translator bias or belief.

47

In Mark 16:9, simply repositioning the first comma dramatically alters the implication of the text:

> Now when Jesus was risen, early the first [day] of the week He appeared first to Mary [of] Magdalene, out of whom He had cast seven devils.

Notice the text no longer implies the resurrection occurred early Sunday, but rather is neutral as to when Jesus arose and, instead, is applicable to when and to whom He first appeared. The fact the above rendering is accurate and correctly conveys the original intent of the author is evident when taken in conjunction with subsequent verses. Mark writes that first Jesus appeared to Mary of Magdalene early on the first day of the week; second, Jesus appeared to two disciples in the countryside; and third, Jesus appeared to *"the Eleven"* apostles during the evening meal. Thus, Mark's emphasis is clearly on the numerous witnesses to whom the resurrected Savior appeared; not the day of the week upon which the resurrection came to pass:

> [9]Now when Jesus was risen, early the first [day] of the week He appeared first to Mary [of] Magdalene, out of whom He had cast seven devils. [10][And] she went and told them that had been with Him, as they mourned and wept. [11]And they, when they had heard that He was alive, and had been seen of her, believed not.

¹²After that, He appeared in another form unto two of them as they walked and went into the country. ¹³And they went and told [it] unto the residue: neither believed they them.

¹⁴Afterward He appeared unto the Eleven as they sat at meat, and upbraided them with their unbelief and hardness of heart, because they believed not them which had seen Him after He was risen.

When set in its proper context, it's apparent the *Gospel of Mark* doesn't chronicle Jesus' resurrection per se, but paraphrases three encounters detailed in the other Gospel accounts wherein Jesus appeared post-resurrection to disciples on the first day of the week; although they weren't believed.

Sabbath Following the Day of Crucifixion

A foundational tenet in determining the day of the crucifixion is the day following was a Sabbath. After all, such is the reason their deaths were expedited and their bodies taken down from the execution-stakes. The Western mindset surmises the Sabbath to be Saturday, and so the crucifixion logically seems to have occurred on Friday. However, in additional to the weekly Sabbath, God ordained seven annual Sabbaths; technically *Appointed Times,*[73] but

---

[73] Leviticus 2:3

usually referred to as *high Sabbaths, high days,* and *high Holy Days.* In like fashion of Christmas and Halloween, these Sabbaths occur on specific days of the year as opposed to a specific day of the week.

The *Gospel of John* specifically labels the Sabbath following Passover as a *"high day."*[74] This is an indisputable indication of it being an annual Sabbath; not the weekly Sabbath. God commands that Passover -- the day Jesus was crucified -- be kept on the 14th day of the first month,[75] and commands that the year's first high Sabbath be observed on the 15th day of the first month.[76] Consequently, the belief Jesus was necessarily crucified on Friday due to the following day being a Sabbath is faulty logic: the day following Passover is always a Sabbath, regardless of the day of the week!

Day of Preparation

The day preceding a Sabbath is known as the *day of preparation* (or *preparation day*), and is when all customary work normally done on the following day is completed in addition to the current day's tasks. Chores such as cooking, cleaning, gardening, and shopping are all prohibited on *the Sabbath*; therefore, the day of preparation is essentially a day of double duty. Sabbath meals, for example,

---

[74] John 19:31
[75] Leviticus 23:5
[76] Leviticus 23:6-7

are prepared on the day before while dishes are done on the day after.

God ordained the seventh day -- Saturday -- as the weekly Sabbath in commemoration of creation; thus, every Friday is a day of preparation. Similarly, annual Sabbaths are also preceded by a day of preparation. Several Gospels mention Jesus being crucified on the *day of preparation*;[77] however, the *Gospel of John* explicitly states *"it was the Preparation of the Passover."*[78] This is definitive proof Jesus was crucified on the day of preparation preceding an annual Sabbath.

Strictly speaking, *the Passover* pertains to the lamb sacrificed for the remission of sins on the 14th day of the first month. John's terminology, *"it was the Preparation of the Passover,"* pertains to the day when the lamb is prepared and sacrificed; not to the day before the sacrifice as if *Passover* were a high Sabbath requiring its own preparation day.

Reference to *the Passover* is understood to also pertain to the day of sacrifice: evening to evening on the 14th day of the first month (the month of the *Abib*,[79] referring to a stage of barley ripeness). Therefore, *the Passover* -- both the sacrifice and the date -- is synonymous with the preparation day for the high Sabbath commencing the Feast of Unleavened Bread on the 15th day in the month of the *Abib*.

---

[77] Mark 15:42; Luke 23:54
[78] John 19:14; see also 19:31 and 19:42
[79] The modern reference to the first month of the Biblical calendar is *Nisan;* derived during the Babylonian exile.

At the same time, the term *Passover* has culturally evolved to encompass the entire eight day span of both the preparation day and the seven-day Feast of Unleavened Bread.[80] As a result, all cultural references to "observing Passover" and "Passover Season" inherently include the Feast of Unleavened Bread. The two occasions go together hand and glove; the high Sabbath commencing the Feast of Unleavened Bread on the 15th must be preceded by the preparation day on the 14th.

As the sun sets on the preparation day known as Passover, the year's first high Sabbath commencing the Feast of Unleavened Bread begins. The Passover meal, known as the *Seder,* is served at evening on the high Sabbath. The whole family congregates around the table, there's a recounting of the Passover story, and the Passover lamb is consumed with bitter herbs, unleavened bread, and wine.

Jesus explained this wine to be symbolic of His blood and the unleavened bread to be symbolic of His body, as He -- the Passover Lamb of God – would be prepared and sacrificed on the 14th day in the month of the *Abib* for the remission of humanity's sins.

The seventh and final day of the Feast of Unleavened Bread, the 21st day in the month of the *Abib,* is the year's second high Sabbath.[81] Therefore, the 20th day in the month of the *Abib* is likewise a preparation day. All work which must be done in preparation for the high Sabbath that concludes the Feast of

---

[80] *Encyclopedia Judaica*, Volume 13, page169; see Luke 22:1
[81] Leviticus 23:6-8; Deuteronomy 16:8

Unleavened Bread is accomplished on this day. And so it is with every preparation day for both weekly- and high Sabbaths.

Removing the Bodies for the Sabbath

Death by crucifixion is an excruciating and prolonged process typically spanning several days before its victim succumbs. Strategically located where locals could view the spectacle day after day as they went about their usual routines, crucifixions were utilized as a public display of Roman power. The condemned was naked,[82] humiliated, and often spat upon and mocked. Romans never crucified Romans,[83] and Hebrews never liked seeing Hebrews crucified; therefore, Jesus' crucifixion at the request of the Jewish leadership is indicative of exceptional hatred.

With Roman occupation already a volatile situation, Israel's Sabbaths were tolerated. Rome typically refrained from antagonizing their Hebrew subjects by littering the landscape with crucifixions during the high Holy Days, particularly around Jerusalem when the city swelled with religious pilgrims.

Jesus' sudden crucifixion was a revolting disturbance in an otherwise joyous occasion. The Jewish leaders' participation in lieu of tending to the festival's attendees was a sacrilege, and the crucifixion's timing amid preparations for the high Sabbath

---

[82] The thighs being exposed was considered naked, so it's unknown whether He was completely uncovered.

[83] Romans citizens were exempt by law except in cases of treason.

when the bodies needed to be removed from the execution-stakes was in extraordinarily poor taste.

> *The Jews therefore, because it was the Preparation [day of the Passover], that the bodies should not remain upon the cross on the Sabbath day [starting at sunset], for that Sabbath day was an high day [Feast of Unleavened Bread], besought Pilate that their legs might be broken, and they might be taken away. (John 19:31)*

Scripture records three men were crucified that day; Jesus along with a thief to His left and to His right.[84] Though Jesus endured six agonizing hours before bowing His head and giving up the ghost, what would customarily be a more prolonged ordeal was expedited so their bodies wouldn't remain crucified during the high Sabbath.

Known as *crucifracture*, the Roman soldiers broke the legs of the two thieves which prevented them from pushing downward upon their feet in order to lift their torso in the

---

[84] Matthew 27:38; Mark 15:27; Luke 23:33; John 19:18

course of breathing. Death occurred within minutes via asphyxiation.

Yet when the soldiers approached Jesus, they saw He was already dead and so His legs were never broken. Instead, as affirmation, a lance was thrust in through His side and upwards into His heart.[85] The three corpses were then removed from the execution-stakes and hurriedly buried or otherwise disposed before nightfall when the high Sabbath commencing the Feast of Unleavened Bread began.

Starting upon the moment Jesus was enclosed within the tomb, marked by the rolling of the large stone over the entrance at twilight when the Sabbath was beginning, He would remain in the heart of the earth for three days and three nights; arising from the dead at precisely that same moment 72-hours later on Saturday.

And so it would be, the Lord of the Sabbath[86] was raised on the Sabbath!

---

[85] John 19:23-33
[86] Matthew 12:8, Mark 2:28, and Luke 6:5

Chapter Four
Day of Messiah's Crucifixion

For thou wilt not leave my soul in hell;
neither wilt thou suffer thine Holy One to see corruption.
(Psalms 16:10)

The Day of Crucifixion and Burial

Knowing that Jesus was crucified on the Passover, i.e. preparation day for the Feast of Unleavened Bread, and knowing that Jesus was resurrected at evening on Saturday after three days and three nights in the heart of the earth, then determining the day of the week when Passover came to pass is simply a matter of counting to three.

Counting backwards, Saturday evening to Friday evening is *one*, Friday evening to Thursday evening is *two*, and Thursday evening to Wednesday evening is *three*. It's that easy. Messiah was crucified Wednesday morning, died Wednesday afternoon, and entombed Wednesday evening!

While a Wednesday crucifixion initially rubs the ears wrong, the Gospels provide ample evidence to substantiate this to be factual and true. The record of dual Sabbaths, Temple guards, the sealing of the tomb, and multiple groups of women at the tomb all corroborate Jesus' Wednesday crucifixion, death, and burial.

Dual Sabbaths

As are most annual commemorations, high Sabbaths are fixed to a specific day of the year as opposed to a specific day of the week. As a result, certain weeks necessarily contain two Sabbaths; a weekly as well as a high (annual). The first day of the Feast of Unleavened Bread, the 15th day of the first month, is the year's first high Sabbath.[87] Therefore, the third week of God's calendar year always entails dual Sabbaths: the first day of the Feast of Unleavened Bread, and Saturday. Consequently, there were two Sabbaths amid the week Jesus was crucified: the high Sabbath following the day of His crucifixion, and the weekly Sabbath preceding the women's arrival at His tomb.

The fact there were dual Sabbaths is conveyed within the Greek text of Matthew 28:1, but it's typically lost in translation. The word from which *"Sabbath"* is derived is plural, *όαββατων* or *sabbaton* (Strong's #G4521); thus, the verse correctly reads, *"At the end of the Sabbaths..."*[88] In context, the verse pertains to Mary of Magdalene and Mary the mother of James arriving at the tomb early Sunday (Saturday after sundown), but is indicative of two Sabbaths transpiring between Joseph of Arimathea enclosing Jesus' body inside the tomb and the angel revealing Jesus is risen and gone!

---

[87] Leviticus 23:6-7

[88] *Green's Literal Translation, Ferrar Fenton's Translation,* and *Alfred Marshall's Parallel New Testament in Greek and English* all render Matthew 28:1 as "after the Sabbaths." *The SCRIPTURES, International Standard Version, Young's Literal Translation,* and the *Complete Word Study Dictionary: New Testament* all acknowledge the duality of *Sabbaths.*

At the end of the Sabbath[s], as it began to dawn[89] toward the first day of the week, Mary [of] Magdalene and the other Mary go to see the sepulcher. (Matthew 28:1, emphasis added)

Naturally, there's a one in seven chance a high Sabbath will coincide with the weekly Sabbath. Nevertheless, Scripture clarifies this is not the case amid the week of Jesus' crucifixion. Comparing the *Gospel of Mark*, wherein the women purchase spices after the Sabbath, with the *Gospel of Luke*, wherein the women prepare spices before the Sabbath, constitutes definitive proof of two separate Sabbaths:

And when the [high] Sabbath was past, Mary [of] Magdalene, Mary the mother of James, and Salome, had bought sweet spices, that they might come and anoint Him. (Mark 16:1)

[After buying them] ...they returned, and prepared spices and ointments; and rested the [weekly] Sabbath day according to the commandment. (Luke 23:56)

It means the women bought and prepared spices on a day that fell between two Sabbaths!

---

[89] Aramaic literally reads *"b'ramsha din b'shabata"* or "in the evening of the Shabbat". The literal meaning of *ramsha* is "evening" or *erev,* but here it is used idiomatically... A more literal form, *"mitil d'shabata aiala",* would be read as "the Sabbath was beginning/ entering/ coming about" (Andrew Gabriel Roth, *Netzari Aramaic English Interlinear*).

Systematically fitting the pieces together, there's the day Jesus was crucified, followed by the high Sabbath, followed by the day the women bought and prepared spices, followed by the weekly Sabbath; Wednesday, Thursday, Friday, and Saturday.

Then, at evening on Saturday, Mary of Magdalene and Mary the mother of James arrive at the tomb whereupon the earth begins to quake; Jesus is risen and then departs through the stone surroundings; an angel from heaven descends and rolls aside the large stone; the guards are terrified and become like dead men; the angel sits upon the stone, proclaims Jesus to be alive, and invites the women to peer inside to see that it's empty!

Lastly, at sunrise the next morning, some Galilean women who are oblivious to the events of the previous evening venture to the tomb intending to anoint Jesus' corpse, but arrive to find the large stone is already rolled aside.

72-Hours in the Heart of the Earth

Wednesday	Thursday	Friday	Saturday	Sunday
Passover: Last Supper, Jesus arrested, crucified, dead, and buried	**High Sabbath: Feast of Unleavened Bread;** no work is done	Women buy and prepare the spices intended to anoint the corpse	**Weekly Sabbath:** women again rest, Jesus is resurrected at evening	Multiple groups of women arrive to find the tomb is empty

(Days are reckoned from evening to evening)

Delay in Anointing the Body

A question often raised is: if the crucifixion occurred on Wednesday, then why did the women wait until Sunday to anoint the body? The answer, in large part, is due to the dual Sabbaths and their inability to work on those days, but it's also due to the tomb being sealed and access forbidden.

A day-by-day overview (formatted according to the familiar midnight to midnight reckoning) makes this plain:

> **Tuesday:** from the Mount of Olives, Jesus sends two disciples ahead to prepare the evening meal. As the sun sets, Jesus and the Twelve partake in the Last Supper.[90] Later that night, while praying in the garden of Gethsemane, Jesus is betrayed by Judas who is accompanied by a detachment of soldiers sent to arrest Him. Jesus is taken before the chief priests,[91] elders, and scribes who have all convened for the purpose of finding reason to put Him to death.[92]

> **Wednesday:** Passover -- Jesus is delivered to Pontius Pilate, the Roman *Prefect of Judaea*, who ultimately complies with the Jewish leaderships' request for crucifixion.[93] Around 9 AM, Jesus is nailed to the

---

[90] Matthew 26:17-29; Mark 14:12-25; Luke 22:8-38; John 13-14
[91] The ranking Levites within each division of priests
[92] Matthew 26:36-27:1; Mark 14:32-55; Luke 22:40-48; John 18:1-3
[93] Matthew 27:11-31; Mark 15:1-15; Luke 23:1-25; John 18:28-19:16

execution-stake; six hours later, He cries out with a loud voice and dies. That evening, as Wednesday draws to a close, His corpse is laid inside the tomb and a large stone is rolled across the entrance enclosing Him.[94]

Thursday: Feast of Unleavened Bread — it's a high Sabbath, and no customary work is done.[95] Mary of Magdalene, the apostles, and others spend the day grieving. Meanwhile, in violation of the Sabbath, chief priests and Pharisees approach Pilate so as to persuade him that Jesus' tomb should be sealed and guarded for the remainder of the three days and three nights.[96]

Friday: women purchase spices and perfumes which they prepare for use in anointing the body.[97] The preparation process is lengthy, and requires much of the day. Between chores from yesterday's high Sabbath, buying and preparing the spices, and preparations for tomorrow's Sabbath, the women have a busy day. Attempting to anoint the corpse would prove difficult, but perhaps not impossible. The ultimate hindrance is the tomb has been sealed by Roman authorities and access is forbidden until the completion of the third day. They have no choice; they must wait until after the weekly Sabbath.

---

[94] Matthew 27:45-60; Mark 15:25-46; Luke 23:44-55
[95] Exodus 12:15-16; Leviticus 23:6-7
[96] Matthew 27:62-66
[97] Mark 16:1; Luke 23:56

> **Saturday:** weekly Sabbath -- everyone again rests per the fourth commandment.[98] At evening, when the Sabbath concludes, Mary of Magdalene and Mary the mother of James venture to the tomb. As they arrive, there's an earthquake and then an angel from heaven rolls aside the stone. The angel informs them of the Good News: Jesus is risen![99] They hurry off to tell the others gathered in the upper-room, but aren't believed.

> **Sunday:** while it was permissible to anoint Jesus' body the previous evening, outside it was cold[100] and dark. With the notable exception of Mary of Magdalene and Mary the mother of James, the women opt to go to the tomb this morning. They arrive at sunrise, and find the stone is already rolled away. Two angels appear and proclaim the Good News: He is risen, and then instruct the women to go relay the information to His disciples, especially Peter.[101]

Factoring in the Guards

Irrespective of the time constraints caused by the Sabbaths and the preparation of burial spices, anyone who attempted to roll away the large stone and gain access to Jesus' corpse

---

[98] Luke 23:56
[99] Matthew 28:1-6
[100] John 18:18
[101] Mark 16:2-7; Luke 24:2-9

would've been physically restrained. The reason is that on Thursday -- the high Sabbath -- the chief priests and Pharisees approached Pontius Pilate with concerns someone might steal the corpse and falsely claim Jesus to be alive. As a result, Pilate consented to the sealing of the tomb and the posting of guards.[102] After that, anyone breaking the seals prior to Sunday (Saturday evening) was subject to immediate arrest.

The seals most likely consisted of a cord stretched across the face of the rolling stone and affixed to both sides of the entrance with clay or wax (alternatively, one side may have been anchored by a spike driven into the stone-facing). The affixation point(s) were then imprinted with the Seal of Rome. The imprint represented all of the power and authority of the Roman Empire. To break the seal was an act punishable by death.

Although the events of Thursday are not fully recounted in Scripture, protocol suggests the following: the Jewish leadership is distraught over the previous day's developments, and so in violation of the high Sabbath they approach Pilate to request Jesus' tomb be sealed and guarded. Pilate consents, and a Roman or Temple official accompanies the assigned guards to the tomb. Upon arriving, they roll aside the large stone to verify Jesus' corpse is still present. Next, they re-roll

---

[102] Matthew 27:65

the large stone over the entrance, stretch a cord across its face, and affix both ends to the surrounding rock; either both ends with clay or wax, or one end with a spike and the other with clay or wax. Lastly, the official uses his Roman signet to imprint the affixation point(s) with the Seal of Rome whereupon he leaves the assigned guards to enforce the decree through the completion of the third day.

The guards themselves do not possess the Roman signet and are unable to re-seal the tomb. It's not within their discretion to break the seals and roll aside the stone in allowing someone to enter. Their job, exclusively, is to ensure the seal(s) remain unbroken. For this reason, the guards effectively bear witness to the fact that Jesus' corpse was present within the tomb on Thursday and that nobody thereafter entered the tomb prior to the two Marys' arrival on Saturday evening.

The Guards' Contrived Story

After encountering the angel and fleeing in fear, the guards went into the city and informed the chief priests. A council was immediately convened, and it was decided the official story would be that Jesus' disciples came and stole His corpse during the night while the guards slept. The guards were paid a sizable sum to convey this false testimony, and they were assured they'd be found blameless should their derelict of duty become known to the governor.[103]

---

[103] Matthew 28:11-15

Alas, the sanctioned propaganda that Jesus' corpse had been stolen by His disciples sometime Friday during the night was circulated among the festival's attendees. The contrived story most likely entailed the guards, upon awakening, ascertaining evidence such as multiple footprints around the large stone and perhaps a trickle of blood leading away from the alleged crime-scene. Furthermore, the guards would've claimed they conducted a thorough investigation before departing their post in order to report the theft to their superiors.

Aside from Mary of Magdalene and Mary the mother of James, nobody else witnessed the guards present at the tomb on Saturday; for everyone observed the Sabbath command. Moreover, in those days women's testimony wasn't considered reliable, so the fact the two Marys had seen the guards at their post Saturday evening -- not to mention quaking in fear and fleeing the scene -- was of no concern.

The other option the council would've contemplated was claiming the guards fulfilled their three day assignment and departed without incident; thereby implying Jesus' corpse was taken at some point afterwards. Yet to claim His corpse was stolen Friday night was to preempt the factual events of the following evening and to best discredit any claim He is risen. After all, if the authorities are stating His corpse was stolen Friday night, who would believe a couple of emotionally distraught, unreliable women alleging an angelic encounter on Saturday evening?!

The Significance of 72 Hours

Jesus' stated duration of *"three days and three nights in the heart of the earth"* was more significant to first-century Hebrews than people may realize. Foremost, at that time, superstition held that the spirit wouldn't depart the body until after three days and the onset of decomposition. The rabbinic *Baraita of Semahorh* reads: "One should go to the cemetery to check the dead within three days and not fear that such smacks of pagan practices; it once happened that a (buried) man was once visited and went on to live another twenty-five years."[104]

This belief is evident in the episode wherein a man named *Jairus* pleaded with Jesus to lay hands on his daughter who died shortly before His arrival. The Pharisees probably reasoned the girl's spirit returned of its own accord, and Jesus was falsely claiming credit; although they publicly denied the girl had ever died and likely invoked Jesus' own words when He metaphorically said *"the damsel is not dead, but sleepeth."*[105] So not only was the miracle denied, but the spectacle was twisted to imply deception.

When Lazarus died, Jesus intentionally delayed His arrival into Bethany until the fourth day.[106] Being past the three day period, and by then *"he stinketh,"*[107] there could be no

---

[104] *Baraita of Semahorh* 8:1
[105] Mark 5:22-39
[106] John 11:6
[107] John 11:39

accusation that Lazarus wasn't truly dead. In fact, because of its undeniable authenticity, people thereafter flocked to see the man who'd been raised back to life. This incident proved so problematic to the Pharisees that they eventually sought reason to put both Lazarus and Jesus to death.[108]

Conversely, in the case of Jesus, dying Friday afternoon and arising Sunday morning wouldn't constitute a valid sign; for it would fall more in the realm of fortuitous resuscitation. Conjuring His resurrection as proof of anything would raise suspicions of a hoax ala *The Passover Plot*[109] and *Holy Blood, Holy Grail.*[110] Yet a full 72-hours entombed in the heart of the earth is irrefutable proof. Thereafter, the only reasonable objection would be skepticism as to Jesus truly being alive; which is probably one reason He appeared to over 500 people in the weeks following His resurrection.[111]

> Jargon clarification: *"in the heart of the earth"* refers to Jesus' corpse being enclosed within the tomb; not His soul descending into the depths of hell. Although Jesus was entombed Wednesday evening through Saturday evening, He had died several hours prior; meaning He was dead in excess of 72-hours -- closer to 75-hours. Like Lazarus, Jesus was dead into the fourth day; but

---

[108] John 12:9-11

[109] Hugh J. Schonfield, *The Passover Plot: A New Light on the History of Jesus* (New York: Bantam, 1965), p. 165.

[110] Michael Baigent, Richard Leigh, and Henry Lincoln, *Holy Blood, Holy Grail* (New York: Delacorte, 1982), p. 372.

[111] 1 Corinthians 15:6

unlike Lazarus, His corpse hadn't started to decompose.[112] This seems to have been averted by having His head and feet anointed in the days prior,[113] Nicodemus packing Him with 100 pounds of myrrh and aloes,[114] and the weather being notably cool.[115]

Third Day Since These Things Were Done

On Sunday afternoon following Jesus' resurrection, two disciples walked out on the fellowship of believers assembled in the upper-room in Jerusalem, and were traveling toward a town called Emmaus; about a seven mile journey. As they walked, they conversed about the unprecedented events of the previous week. At some point along the way Jesus joined them, though they didn't recognize who He is. Jesus then inquired about the things they were discussing. The 24th chapter of Luke records their response:

> [19]...And they said unto Him, concerning Jesus of Nazareth, which was a prophet mighty in deed and word before God and all the people, [20]and how our chief priests and our rulers delivered Him to be condemned to death, and have crucified Him. [21]But we trusted that it had been

---

[112] Psalms 16:10
[113] Matthew 26:7; Mark 14:3; John 12:3
[114] John 19:39-40
[115] John 18:18

He which should have redeemed Israel. And beside all this, <u>today is the third day since these things were done</u>. ²²Yea, and certain women also of our company made us astonished which were early at the sepulcher; ²³and when they found not His body, they came, saying, that they had also seen a vision of angels which said that He was alive.

Notice they said *"the third day since these things were done"* as opposed to *"the third day since His crucifixion."* Notice also that Luke earlier explains *"they were talking with each other about <u>all</u> the things that had taken place."*[116] As the three of them walked, the disciples would have detailed everything: how on Monday the Sanhedrin plotted to have Him arrested; how on Tuesday Judas was bribed to betray Him; how on Wednesday He was scourged and crucified, Joseph of Arimathea secured custody of the body, and at evening when the high Sabbath was beginning Joseph enclosed Him in a new tomb; and how on Thursday the Jewish leadership, still not satisfied, had the tomb sealed and guards posted through the completion of the third day.

It's at this point that *"today is the third day <u>since</u> these things were done"* is in context. Sunday constitutes the third day since Joseph of Arimathea rolled the large stone across the tomb's entrance, and since the tomb was sealed and guarded.

---

[116] Luke 24:14, emphasis added

The word translated *"since"* is derived from the Greek word ἀπό or *apo* (Strong's #G575). It literally means 'of separation' and in this case is applicable to the 'temporal, of distance of time.' It affirms the two disciples' verbiage didn't pertain to the third day inclusive of Sunday, but to three days prior to Sunday.

Three days prior to Sunday -- whether referring to three days in full by corresponding to Jesus' entombment at evening as the high Sabbath was beginning, or referring to three days in part by corresponding to the tomb being sealed and guarded -- is inescapably a reference to Thursday.

Several Bible translations are faithful to the source manuscripts in relaying this aspect of terminology when rendering the verse in English:

Moffatt, New Translation (MNT) --
> *...but He is dead, and that is three days ago!*

The Berkeley Version in Modern English (BV) --
> *Moreover, three days have already passed since all these events occurred.*

The distinction is likewise evident within Aramaic translations which are preserved in the Syraic Reading of ancient manuscripts known as the *Sinaitic Palimpset* and the *Curetonian Syriac*. They are rendered into English as follows:

The Syriac New Testament Translated Into English From The Peshitto[117] --

> *... and lo, three days have passed since all these things occurred.*

In its proper context, the implication of Luke 24:21 is that Sunday constitutes the third day of separation from the day when *"these things were done,"* i.e. the entombment of Jesus, and the sealing and guarding of the tomb. However, Jesus was crucified on the day before *"these things were done,"* so His death exceeded the three day threshold. In the same manner as Lazarus, Jesus was dead into the fourth day!

With the rising of the sun on the first day of the week, more than three days of separation since Jesus' entombment had passed. As a result, the seals had expired and mourners were permitted to enter. Consequently, a group of Galilean women ventured to the tomb intending to properly anoint the corpse with burial spices, but quickly returned to the upper-room with a startling claim of finding the large stone rolled aside, the tomb to be empty, and angels proclaiming Jesus to be alive!

In recounting facets of the two disciples' conversation, Luke affirms the full 72-hour duration of Jesus' entombment by relaying their bewilderment as to the tomb being empty after such a length of time. Essentially the disciples were saying, 'Jesus has now been dead in excess of three days and three

---

[117] The traditional New Testament of the *Peshitta* has 22 books, lacking 2 John, 3 John, 2 Peter, Jude, and Revelation, which are books of the *Antilegomena*. The text of Gospels also lacks the *"Pericope Adulterae;"* which is John 7:53-8:11 and Luke 22:17-18.

nights; so, while we know it's impossible, there are reports He's alive!' These despondent disciples were not ignorant of the fact Jesus was past the point of no return, and therefore refused to believe the women's account even to the point of walking out on the assembly in the upper-room.

Yet Jesus is not willing that any of His sheep should go astray, and personally set out to bring them back into the fold. They knew His voice -- their hearts burned within them as He spoke[118] -- and after Jesus broke bread among them, they quickly returned to the assembly in Jerusalem.

Mark's Account of Galilean Women

The fact that Sunday commenced the fourth day since Jesus' entombment as well as since the sealing of the tomb and the posting of guards is further corroborated in the *Gospel of Mark* which entails the account of Galilean women on their way to the tomb at sunrise. This group of women, separate and distinct from Mary of Magdalene and Mary the mother of James, is initially concerned with who they'll find to roll aside the large stone in order to anoint the corpse.[119]

---

[118] Luke 24:32
[119] Mark 16:2-3

The act of enclosing Jesus' tomb consisted of rolling a large disc-shaped boulder down a slanted groove and lodging it into place in front of the entrance. Though easy to roll down, it typically required several men to roll back up. For this reason, after the seals expired and the guards were gone, the women were permitted to enter and anoint the corpse provided they could get past the large stone enclosing the tomb.

This is significant because if Sunday had commenced the third day since Jesus' entombment, then the women would've presumed the guards to still be there. And if the guards were still there, then the women would've anticipated those guards, under penalty of death, to forbid the seals from being broken. Hence, the women wouldn't have been concerned with *who* was going to roll aside the stone so much as with *how* they were going to persuade the guards to commit a capital offense in allowing the large stone to be rolled aside.

The very fact these women ventured to the tomb intending to anoint the corpse demonstrates the third day since Jesus' entombment had come and gone. The women clearly knew three days had past and the seals had expired, they knew the guards' assignment was over and they had departed, and they knew they were able to access the tomb free and clear of legal consequence presuming they could find someone capable of rolling the large stone up and out of the way.

For reasons of chronology, It's important to understand that these Galilean women, as of sunrise, were still oblivious to the astonishing events witnessed by the two Marys during the previous evening; for had these women known an angel from heaven already rolled aside the stone, they would've never been concerned with who was going to do so. Moreover, had these women known that Mary of Magdalene and Mary the mother of James had been there some 12-hours earlier, they would've also known the tomb was empty and so never wasted their time bringing burial spices in the first place!

Nevertheless, this group of women arrives at the tomb Sunday morning and are surprised to find the stone already rolled aside. They then enter the tomb and are frightened by an angel near the place where the Lord's body had laid (as opposed to sitting upon the large stone outside of the entrance as was the case the precious evening):

> And entering into the sepulchre, they saw a young
> man sitting on the right side, clothed in a long
> white garment; and they were affrighted. And he
> saith unto them, "Be not affrighted. Ye seek Jesus
> of Nazareth, which was crucified; He is risen! He is
> not here! Behold the place where they laid Him."
> (Mark 16:5-6)

Furthermore, exhibiting behavior opposite of the two Marys who were obedient to the angel's instructions to tell Peter and the others, this particular group of women flees in fear and says nothing to anyone.[120]

---

[120] Mark 16:8

Historic Advocacy

History proclaims that Good Friday – Easter Sunday is fictitious; it didn't happen. It appears to be Biblical, but it's deception. It masquerades as factual, yet it's fabricated. It seems authentic, however, it's counterfeit. Behind the façade of 1700 years of coerced adherence, the Good Friday – Easter Sunday tradition is nothing more than a cleverly devised fable which substitutes myth in place of truth.

Jesus' "Last Supper" occurred on Tuesday, His crucifixion on Wednesday, the high Sabbath beginning the Feast of Unleavened Bread on Thursday, the women bought and prepared spices on Friday, the weekly Sabbath observed on Saturday, and the tomb discovered empty on Sunday.

After remaining in the heart of the earth from Wednesday evening through Saturday evening, Jesus again took up His life.[121] Thereafter, He appeared to several of His disciples at various times on First-fruits Sunday before manifesting to the group gathered in the upper-room that evening.

This is not new revelation, but a long-standing position advocated by several Church Fathers including Epiphanus of Salamis (inter c. 310–320 – 403),[122] Victorinus of Pettau (died c. 303 or 304 CE),[123] Lactantius (c. 240 – 320),[124] Cassiodorus (c. 485 – 585),[125] and Gregory of Tours (c. 538 – 594).[126]

---

[121] John 10:17-18
[122] http://en.wikipedia.org/wiki/Epiphanius_of_Salamis
[123] http://en.wikipedia.org/wiki/Victorinus_of_Pettau

More recent proponents of the Wednesday crucifixion include Westcott (c. 1825 – 1901),[127] R.A. Torrey (c. 1856 – 1928),[128] Finis Dake (c. 1902 – 1987),[129] Herbert W. Armstrong (c. 1892 – 1986),[130] Chuck Missler,[131] Kent Hovind,[132] and Michael Rood.[133]

[124] http://en.wikipedia.org/wiki/Lactantius

[125] http://en.wikipedia.org/wiki/Cassiodorus

[126] http://en.wikipedia.org/wiki/Gregory_of_Tours

[127] http://en.wikipedia.org/wiki/Brooke_Westcott

[128] http://en.wikipedia.org/wiki/R._A._Torrey

[129] http://en.wikipedia.org/wiki/Finis_Jennings_Dake

[130] http://en.wikipedia.org/wiki/Herbert_W._Armstrong

[131] http://khouse.org/pages/mcat/khouse/about_the_misslers/

[132] http://www.creationtoday.org/about/dr-kent-hovind/

[133] http://michaelrood.tv/about-michael-rood

Chapter Five

Typology and Shadow-pictures

Who serve unto the example and
shadow of heavenly things... (Hebrews 8:5)

Scriptural Patterns and Cyclical Reckoning

Humans have a tendency to situate events chronologically along a time-line running left to right, and to designate each with a specific beginning and end; however, the perspective of Scripture is cyclical. Like phases of the moon, seasons of the year, and the circle of life, so themes and patterns of Scripture occur in repeating fashion.

Those who don't know history are doomed to repeat it: the success and failure of businesses, the gain and loss of liberty, and the rise and fall of nations. Each is predicated upon similar circumstances; *the handwriting on the wall,* so to speak. People are creatures of habit, one's days become a familiar routine, and every generation essentially shares the same experiences. *"There is no new [thing] under the sun."*[134]

While history teaches that man learns nothing from history, the student of Scripture is without excuse. God relays His instructions of righteousness through His laws and precepts,

---

[134] Ecclesiastes 1:9

He previews His plan of redemption through the high Sabbaths, and He shares the history and travails of a stiff-necked people so that believers are not found to be ignorant of lessons of the past.

> *Now all these things happened unto them for examples: and they are written for our admonition, upon whom the ends of the [age] are come. (1 Corinthians 10:11)*

Identifying patterns within this cyclical characteristic of Scripture is known as *typology* -- the study of types, models, figures, and shadow-pictures. It proves enlightening to analyze how people and events throughout the Hebrew Bible (Old Testament) serve as pretexts for grander manifestations within the life of Messiah. In recognition of this, typology can cautiously be used as a validating attribute. In so doing, there are shadow-pictures throughout Scripture which serve to reaffirm the *"three days and three nights"* that Jesus was entombed in the heart of the earth.

Jesus personally attested to these shadow-pictures when He appeared post-resurrection to two of His disciples walking along the road to Emmaus:

> *Then opened He their understanding, that they might understand the Scriptures, and said unto them, "Thus it is written, and thus it behooved Christ to suffer, and to rise from the dead the third day." (Luke 24:45-46)*

Jesus clarifies that His suffering, death, and resurrection on the third day are all foretold in the Hebrew Bible; which was the totality of Scripture at the time. So where in the Hebrew Bible are these things written? Jesus had to open their minds in order for them to understand because they're not written verbatim but are typologically found in types, models, and shadow-pictures.

Presented in this chapter are six examples of types, models, and shadow-pictures pertaining to Jesus' duration in the heart of the earth. Those are followed by the typological implications of Jonah as a type of Israel. Typology is a fascinating premise which opens up a new realm of Biblical understanding, and imparts a new appreciation for the awesome God behind the scenes who orchestrates human events amid the crafting of Scripture.

The Shadow-picture in Noah

The Good Friday – Easter Sunday tradition falsely implies Jesus was crucified on Friday, the 14th day of the first month (*Abib*); and resurrected on Sunday, the 16th day of the first month. Yet not only does this negate the *sign of Jonah*, but it breaks the Scriptural model established some 2400 years earlier as found

ABIB						
Sun	Mon	Tue	Wed	Thu	Fri	Sat
						1
2	3	4	5	6	7	8
9	10	11	12	13	14	15
16	17	18	19	20	21	22
23	24	25	26	27	28	29
30						

in the early chapters of Genesis. Forever preserved within the account of Noah and the flood is a foreshadowing of Messiah as it pertains to the day of His resurrection:

> And the ark rested in the seventh month, on the seventeenth day of the month, upon the mountains of Ararat. (Genesis 8:4)

In the days of Noah, God's calendar began in autumn with New Year's occurring on the first day of the month of *Tishri*. Some 900 years later, shortly after Israel's exodus from Egypt, God changed the reckoning of years by making *Tishri* into the seventh month; and the seventh month -- the month of the *Abib* -- into the *"beginning of months."*[135] In other words, the seventh month of the "Civil Calendar" became the first month of the "Religious Calendar."

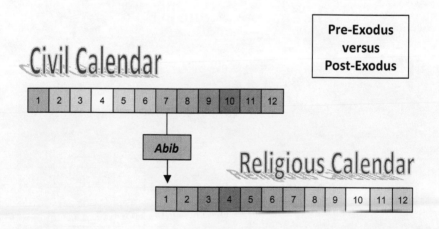

---

[135] Exodus 12:2

It's on the post-Exodus "Religious Calendar" that Passover occurs on the 14th day of the first month.[136] Hence, knowing Jesus was crucified on Passover and then entombed for three

ABIB						
Sun	Mon	Tue	Wed	Thu	Fri	Sat
				1	2	3
4	5	6	7	8	9	10
11	12	13	14	15	16	17
18	19	20	21	22	23	24
25	26	27	28	29	30	

days and three nights, His resurrection necessarily occurred on the 17th day of the first month. Being the 17th day of the first month on the "Religious Calendar" is equivalent to the 17th day of the seventh month on the "Civil Calendar," these two events came to pass on the exact same day.

The shadow-picture is this: just as the world was renewed when Noah's ark came to rest on the 17th day in the month of the *Abib*, so the world was renewed in Messiah when He arose from the dead on the 17th day in the month of the *Abib*!

The Shadow-picture in Abraham and Isaac

One of the most remarkable examples of typology is found in the account of Genesis 22 wherein Abraham is commanded by God Almighty to sacrifice his only son, Isaac. While the concept of human sacrifice is repulsive, this incident in its full Messianic context is a breath-taking shadow-picture of another Father who would sacrifice His only Son as payment in redeeming a sinful humanity.

---

[136] Leviticus 23:5

When Abraham was 99 years old, his wife miraculously became pregnant with Isaac. At age 100, Abraham was thrilled to finally bear a child through his formerly barren wife, Sarah, who was well beyond child-bearing years at age 90. Abraham threw a party when Isaac -- the son of promise -- was weaned, but no further reference to age is given until Sarah's death; when Isaac was 37. At some point in between -- there's no real indication as to when as the word *"lad"* in Hebrew, נער or *na`ar* (Strong's #H5288), also means *'young man'* -- God called upon Abraham in a test of his faith:

> And the LORD said, *"Take now thy son, thine only son Isaac, whom thou lovest, and get thee into the land of Moriah; and offer him there for a burnt offering upon one of the mountains which I will tell thee of."* (Genesis 22:2)

Per God's instruction, Abraham set out the next morning with Isaac, two servants, a donkey, and firewood. After a three day journey, they arrived at the designated mountain. Abraham instructed his two servants to remain with the donkey at the base while he and Isaac ventured up to worship.

It's not a mountain per western concept, but a ridge system between the Mount of Olives and Mount Zion. Ascending from the south, about 600 meters above sea level, Abraham carried the fire and knife while Isaac bore the wood upon his back. Isaac inquired, *"Where is the lamb for the burnt offering?"* Abraham answered, *"God will provide Himself a lamb..."*[137]

---

[137] Genesis 22:7-8

Arriving at the peak -- 777 meters above sea level -- Abraham erected an alter, bound his beloved son, and set him upon the wood. It seems Isaac didn't resist but was obedient to his father's will. As Abraham raised the knife, an angel heralded, *"Lay not thine hand upon the lad, neither do thou any thing unto him: for now I know that thou fearest God, seeing thou hast not withheld thy son, thine only son from Me."*[138]

While some may question Abraham's willingness to comply with such a command, Abraham knew it was not the permanent demise of his son. God had made promises regarding Isaac and the children who would be born to him, so Abraham faithfully obeyed in full expectation of Isaac's resurrection! This is not conjecture, but the assertion of the apostle Paul in his writings to the Messianic Hebrews:

> *By faith Abraham, when he was tried, offered up Isaac: and he that had received the promises offered up his only begotten son, of whom it was said that in Isaac shall thy seed be called: accounting that God was able to raise him up, even from the dead; from whence also he received him in a figure [shadow-picture].*
> *(Hebrews 11:17-19)*

Abraham himself seems to have perceived the entire episode was a rehearsal for some grander future fulfillment. Although a ram caught by its horns in the thicket sufficed for an

---

[138] Genesis 22:12

immediate substitute, it wasn't the lamb that God promised; thus, Abraham knew it wasn't the ultimate fulfillment of the symbolic incident in which they had just participated. Abraham appropriately named the place *Mount Moriah* -- meaning 'the mount ordained by *[YAH]*'[139] -- and then declared *"In the mount of the LORD it shall be seen."*[140]

A thousand years later, Mount Moriah served as the threshing floor for *Ornan*[141] the Jebusite. Located just below the peak at 741 meters above sea level, a prevailing wind facilitated the separation of grain from chaff. At that time, King David provoked God to anger and consequently the destroying angel slaughtered 70,000 Hebrews. This threshing floor on Mount Moriah is where God's anger relented. Therefore, David purchased the land, began offering sacrifices, and determined *"This is [to be the location of] the house of the LORD God, and this is [to be] the Altar of the burnt offering for Israel."*[142]

King David designed the Temple and stockpiled the building materials, but it was his son Solomon who oversaw its construction and completion:

> *Then Solomon began to build the house of the LORD at Jerusalem in Mount Moriah, where the LORD appeared unto David his father, in the place that David had prepared in the threshing-floor of Ornan the Jebusite. (2 Chronicles 3:1)*

---

[139] *YAH* is the poetic form of God's name appearing 53 times
[140] Genesis 22:14
[141] Or *Assaraunah*
[142] 1 Chronicles 22:1

It would be another 800 years before the foretold substitute would come to pass on Mount Moriah -- the Mount ordained by YAH where it shall be seen that *"God will provide Himself a lamb."* It was fulfilled by Jesus of Nazareth, the Lamb of God, when He was led out through the Damascus Gate and north of the city wall[143] to be crucified on the peak of Mount Moriah -- at the precise spot where Abraham intended to sacrifice Isaac; i.e. *Golgotha.*

Both Isaac and Jesus were "only" sons, both were obedient to their father unto death,[144] both carried the wood for the sacrifice upon their back, and both incidents occurred at the exact same location -- the place where God's anger relents and is turned away!

Yet the shadow-picture relevant to the topic at hand pertains to the duration of death. Admittedly the angel stayed Abraham's hand and Isaac never actually died, but this is a type or model, and therefore it incorporates a period of time when Isaac was essentially dead. Scripture records it was the third day of their journey when they went up to worship on Mount Moriah; however, this in itself isn't indication of 72-hours. Nevertheless, God had given Abraham the command to sacrifice Isaac on the day preceding their three day journey, and it was then when Abraham's heart began to mourn his "dead" son. Thus, reckoning from the time of God's command, Isaac is found to have been restored back to "life" after three full days.

---

[143] Hebrews 12:13
[144] Philippians 2:8

The shadow-picture is indeed that of Messiah's three days and three nights in the heart of the earth, as it essentially took 72-hours to play out God's test of Abraham's faith!

Three Full Days

Command	1st Day	2nd Day	3rd Day
Isaac is essentially dead	They set out towards the mount	All day spent traveling	Ascend; Isaac is restored

The Shadow-picture in Rahab

Approximately four hundred years after Abraham, as the Hebrews prepared to cross the Jordan River and take possession of the Promised Land, Joshua sent two spies ahead on a reconnaissance mission. They entered the renowned city of Jericho and lodged with a prostitute named Rahab who received them *"with peace."*[145] Perhaps hoping that entering the house of a prostitute wouldn't attract attention, their presence was nonetheless immediately reported to the king. When authorities arrived to take Rahab in for questioning, the Hebrew spies were hiding among the stalks of flax on her roof. After lying to the king, Rahab returned home whereupon she aided the spies' escape by lowering a cord from the window and allowing them to descend the city wall:

---

[145] Hebrews 11:31

*Then she let them down by a cord through the
window: for her house was upon the town wall,
and she dwelt upon the wall. (Joshua 2:15)*

The word *"cord"* in this verse is derived from the Hebrew word
חבל or *chebel* (Strong's #H2256), which in context means 'rope'
or 'line,' but can also mean 'pain, sorrow, travail.'

After a search-party rode away in pursuit of Rahab's false lead,
she instructed the spies to hide in the mountains for three
days. Then, after the search-party returned to the city, they
were able to safely go on their way:

*And she said unto them, "Get you to the
mountain, lest the pursuers meet you; and hide
yourselves there three days, until the pursuers
be returned: and afterward may ye go your
way." (Joshua 2:16)*

In recompense for her good works,[146] the spies provided Rahab
with a line of scarlet thread which they instructed her to hang
from the window during their siege of the city. Everyone
dwelling within the house marked by the scarlet thread was
promised to be preserved through the destruction:

*Behold, when we [Hebrews] come into the land,
thou shalt bind this line of scarlet thread in the
window which thou didst let us down by: and*

---

[146] James 2:25

> *thou shalt bring thy father, and thy mother, and*
> *thy brethren, and all thy father's household,*
> *home unto thee. (Joshua 2:18-19)*

The word *"thread"* in this verse is derived from the Hebrew word תקוה or *tiqvah (Strong's #H8615),* which in context means 'cord,' but can also mean 'hope, expectation, things hoped for.'

The scarlet thread is an obvious reference [type, model, and shadow-picture] to Messiah's precious blood being a protective marker which affords those dwelling in grace to be preserved through the destruction of man's works.

Yet digging deeper into the text, amid the narrative of the immediate story, Scripture is crafted in such a way whereas the phrase *"three days"* occurs between the words *"cord"* and *"thread."* This is a very subtle shadow-picture showing that *"three days"* occurs between *sorrow* and *travail (חבל or chebel),* and *hope* and *expectation (תקוה or tiqvah).*

Indeed, per the *sign of Jonah*, there were three days between the sorrows and travail of Messiah's Wednesday crucifixion, and the blessed hope and expectation when He appeared to His disciples on First-fruits Sunday!

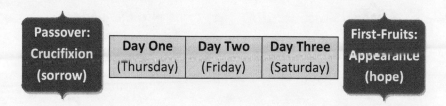

Passover: Crucifixion (sorrow)	Day One (Thursday)	Day Two (Friday)	Day Three (Saturday)	First-Fruits: Appearance (hope)

The Shadow-picture Found in Scarlet

There are two Hebrew words translated into English as "*scarlet.*" They are שני or *shaniy* (Strong's #H8144), and תולע or *towla`* (Strong's #H8438). Among the definitions is *Kermes ilicis,*[147] the insect from where scarlet coloring was historically derived. The two Hebrew words are synonymous and largely interchangeable, and context determines whether it's an adjective relating to its color, or a noun relating to the insect or dye.

The genus *Kermes* is a scale insect, considered 'soft scale' or 'wax scale' due to waxy secretions that coat their soft body. The females are described as "...round, about the size of a pea, contain coloring matter analogous to carmine, and are used in dyeing."[148] They reside in a species of oak trees around the Mediterranean wherein they pierce a thin layer of bark and suck the sap directly from the tree's vascular system. Although long mistaken as part of the vegetation, they eventually came to be commonly referred to as "scarlet worms."

---

[147] Formerly '*coccus ilicis*'; distantly related to the cochineal insect, it originates from the word *kirmizi* meaning "red" in Turkic languages.
[148] "*Coccus ilicis*" - Webster's Revised Unabridged Dictionary from Dictionary.com

The scarlet/crimson dye extracted from these so-called worms was the source of coloring for the scarlet thread bound to the hand of the younger twin who first reached out of Tamar's womb,[149] the scarlet furnishings within the Tabernacle, the scarlet garments of the High Priest, and the line of scarlet thread given to Rahab by the Hebrew spies.

This all becomes significant in light of Jesus, while crucified at Golgotha, declaring Himself to be a type of this worm; foretold in Psalms 22:6 -- *"But I [am] a worm [תּוֹלַע or towla`],[150] and no man; a reproach of men, and despised of the people."* In so doing, Jesus invoked a powerful shadow-picture.

The first similarity is visual association. Isaiah 52:14 states, *"As many were astonished at thee; his visage was so marred more than any man, and his form more [malformed] than the sons of men."* Essentially, Jesus was so beaten and bloodied upon the execution-stake that He was scantly recognizable as human. Likewise, this "scarlet worm" is scarcely recognizable; having been mistaken as vegetation for centuries.

Yet the analogous aspect most striking is that when ready to reproduce, the "worm" permanently affixes herself to a branch or twig. She becomes swollen with eggs and a crimson fluid resembling blood; the stage at which they were harvested. Upon laying her eggs securely beneath her, the crimson fluid oozes from her dying body, covering the eggs and staining the tree. The scarlet worm dies, and the eggs hatch over the next

---

[149] Genesis 38:28-30
[150] Strong #H8438

three days. As her expended corpse dries out, it begins to flake away causing the larvae disperse. On the fourth day, the body is completely gone and only a white spot remains.

> ...though your sins be as scarlet, they shall be as white as snow; though they be red like crimson, they shall be as wool. (Isaiah 1:18)

The scarlet worm literally dies upon the tree, shedding its valuable crimson fluid in order that many may live. Yet the spectacle of the bloody death is erased after three days as the corpse has vanished and the stain becomes white!

The Shadow-picture in Esther

Having previously covered the three day fast within the Scroll of Esther as entailing three 24-hour days,[151] a fascinating shadow-picture emerges in relation to Jesus' appearance in the upper-room on First-fruits Sunday. With Esther approaching King Ahasuerus *"on the third day"* and he accepting her invitation for him and Haman to attend a banquet of wine that evening, it was during that banquet when the three-day and three-night fast came to completion. Thus, while events had been set in motion, their outcome was yet to be revealed.

King Ahasuerus graciously accepted Esther's second invitation for him and Haman to attend another banquet the following

---

[151] Chapter 2, pp. 26-28

evening; essentially 24-hours after the completion of the fast. It was during the following evening's banquet when the Hebrews' deliverance became manifest.

So as Esther, her maidens, and the Hebrews fasted and prayed for deliverance from sunset to sunset for 72-hours, and finally learned their prayers had been answered 24-hours afterwards when their adversary -- who was to slay them all -- was defeated during the second evening's banquet; so the disciples and world anxiously awaited deliverance as Messiah remained in the heart of the earth from sunset to sunset for 72-hours, and finally learned He was risen 24-hours after His resurrection when Jesus revealed Himself during the evening's First-fruits banquet in the upper-room whereupon He proclaimed the adversary -- who was to require the death of them all – had been defeated!

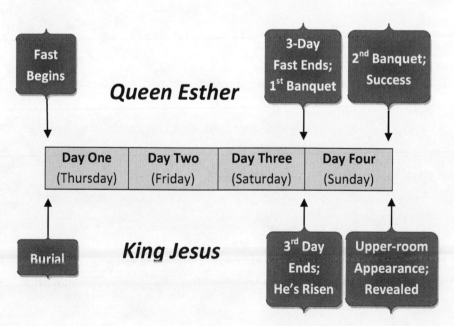

The Shadow-pictures in Jonah

In painting a Scriptural canvas of symbolic pictures, the destiny of the Hebrew people and the embodiment of Messiah is captured like no other within the *Scroll of Jonah*. Beyond the shadow-picture entailing three days and three nights, the abundant typology throughout Jonah is compelling. To study Jonah is to study the types and patterns relevant to both Jesus' ministry and Israel's providence; for the *sign of Jonah* constitutes a great deal more than its 72-hour component.

Jonah's early career was as a beloved prophet of Israel who rightfully foretold several of the king's conquests. Additionally, Jonah prophesied of the restoration of Israel's territory and the expansion of Israel's borders to boundaries not held since the time of King Solomon;[152] up to Hamath (Syria) in the north, and down to the Dead Sea in the south.[153]

Yet following the exile of the kingdom of Israel, Jonah devolved into a prophet of little respect. When Jesus invoked the *sign of Jonah* as proof of being the Messiah, it wasn't received as an endearing allegory. In fact, it probably served to further malign Jesus from the Jewish authorities. When the Sanhedrin later debated whether Jesus was of God, they cynically stated *"...Search, and look: for out of Galilee ariseth no prophet."*[154]

---

[152] 2 Kings 14:25
[153] I Kings 8:65
[154] John 7:52

This wasn't said in ignorance of Jonah's origins, but in disrespect. They effectively stated, 'We don't recognize Jonah as a prophet of God; therefore, per Deuteronomy-13, there's no precedence for the Messiah to come out of the Galilee.'

Jonah was commissioned to preach to the Gentile inhabitants of Nineveh; however, he was so incensed by the idea that he set sail in the opposite direction. Jonah boarded a merchant ship destined for the port of *Tarshish*. This port's location is still a matter of speculation, but many now believe it was in southern Spain. However, this is at odds with Scripture denoting *"...every three years once came the ships of Tarshish bringing gold, and silver, ivory, and apes, and peacocks."*[155] Some two centuries before Jonah, King Solomon commissioned a fleet of ships to sail exclusively to and from *Tarshish*;[156] the roundtrip voyage took three whole years. Moreover, its cargo entailed *"ivory, and apes, and peacocks,"* so *Tarshish* was most likely a port in Africa, India, or Asia.

Jonah 1:3 states, *"...Jonah rose up to flee unto Tarshish from the presence of the* LORD.*"* Obviously it's impossible to flee from the presence of the LORD, so what does this verse really mean? The word *"presence"* stems from the Hebrew word פָּנִים or *paniym,* (Strong's #H6440), which means 'in front of, before, to the front of, in the presence of, in the face of.' Therefore, it means Jonah wanted to get out of God's face; i.e. he fled the region where he could be of service to God. With *Tarshish* located on another continent, the verse makes perfect sense.

---

[155] 1 Kings 10:22 and 2 Chronicles 9:21
[156] 2 Chronicles 20:36

Jonah didn't board some Hebrew freighter on its weekly voyage across the Mediterranean Sea, he boarded a foreign ship destined for the other side of the known world.

The ship set sail from the Judean port of Joppa on the Mediterranean coast.[157] There's no indication as to how far they sailed, but at some point along the route a mighty storm began churning the sea and their vessel took on water. Jonah descended below deck and fell into a deep sleep. He knew the tempest was of God for the purpose of inducing obedience, yet preferred to die rather than comply with God's command. Jonah slept through the tempest until a frantic captain awoke him with the crew in fear for their lives.

When first commissioned to Nineveh, God said to Jonah: *"Arise* [קוּם or *quwm* (Strong's #H6965)]*, go to Nineveh… and cry out* [קְרָא or *qara'* (Strong's #H7121)] *against it."*[158] In this instance, when the captain awoke Jonah, he essentially said the same thing: *"…arise,* [קוּם or *quwm*]*, call* [קְרָא or *qara'*] *upon thy God."*[159] Assuredly Jonah realized the Almighty was utilizing the Gentile captain as a vessel of His message.

The mariners had prayed to their gods for deliverance, but to no avail. They hoped Jonah's God might deliver them. Jonah was uncooperative, so they resorted to casting lots in determining the source of their predicament. When the lot fell upon Jonah, he confessed his situation. In so doing, he

---

[157] Jonah 1:3
[158] Jonah 1:2
[159] Jonah 1:6

introduced his shipmates to God Almighty: Creator of dry ground and sea.[160] The mariners inquired what must be done. Jonah replied that casting him overboard would end the storm.

The mariners refused Jonah's directive and immediately resumed rowing the ship, but the storm worsened. They had no alternative. They prayed to God Almighty that they not be held accountable for Jonah's blood, and then lifted him up and tossed him into the stormy waters. As the prophet foretold, the sea was immediately calmed. The mariners were awe-struck, and thereafter came to worship God Almighty by making vows and later presenting a slaughter offering.[161]

Jonah was quickly swallowed by a great fish; presumably a whale but not necessarily so. The Assyrians were worshippers of Dagon, the fish-god. The Almighty used Jonah to mock the Assyrians' god in like manner as He used Moses to mock the Egyptian gods. Therefore, it's possible Jonah was swallowed by a fish reminiscent of Dagon's contrived appearance.

The Hebrew words, דג גדול or *gadowl dag* (Strong's #H1419 and #H1709), literally mean 'great fish' and therein lend no insight into the issue. Furthermore, at that time, Hebrew had no word specifying 'whale,' nor was it classified as a 'mammal.'

---

[160] Jonah 1:9

[161] Jonah 1:16; they are perhaps source material for Psalms 107:23-31

While in the stomach of the great fish, Jonah was carried down into the depths of the sea. The word *hell* is derived from the Hebrew word שְׁאוֹל or *shĕ'owl* (Strong's #H7592), and was considered to be in the depths of the earth, i.e. the grave, the abyss, the bottomless pit. So amid Jonah's affliction in hell, he cried out to God. Then, after three days and three nights, Jonah was vomited out upon dry ground. From there, Jonah journeyed to Nineveh to forewarn of impending judgment. He afterwards departed the city, erected a booth, and tabernacled in hopes of seeing fire and brimstone rain down upon it.

A miracle in its own right, the Ninevites -- from the king on down -- heeded Jonah's warning. They all repented, and put on sackcloth and ashes. God's anger relented and the city was spared. Jonah, however, was enraged that God hadn't destroyed them, and afterwards pled for God to take his life.

It's a compelling account, yet questions linger. For instance, when the crew tossed Jonah overboard, everyone -- including Jonah -- presumed it was to certain death. Why did Jonah prefer to die rather than comply with God's instruction to preach to the Ninevites? Jonah wasn't some rookie prophet with no desire for his divine calling; to the contrary, he was a recognized prophet throughout the land of Israel. What, then, essentially caused Jonah to resign from the ministry? His actions constitute an astounding act of defiance and disobedience; to this day mocked as a poor example. What's more, after the entire city of Nineveh came to repentance, why did Jonah again plea with God to snuff out his life?

These are underlying issues which belie the superficial rationale of pride, arrogance, and rebellion to which Jonah is commonly attributed. There's clearly more than meets the eye, especially in light of Jesus patterning His ministry after Jonah. There's a wealth of insight to be gained from digging deeper into this matter.

Reconstructed - Mashki Gate

The quest for answers begins with a profiling of Nineveh. Located on the eastern bank of the Tigris River in modern-day Iraq, its first mention is in Genesis 10:11. *"From there [Nimrod] went north to Assyria and built Nineveh..."* Nineveh means 'house of Ninus; or Nimrod;' and the Assyrians were descendants of Assur, the second son of Shem.[162] Nineveh eventually served as the capital of the Assyrian empire, which, by the time of Jonah, had become the dominant world power. Being a mortal enemy of the Hebrew people, the political dealings between their rival kingdoms are recorded in *2 Kings* and *2 Chronicles*.

The Assyrians were a notoriously violent and vicious people. There's a famous poem by Lord Byron which opens: "The Assyrian came down like the wolf on the fold."[163]

---

[162] Genesis 10:22

[163] George Gordon Noel Byron, Lord Byron (1788-1824), *"The Destruction of Sennacherib,"* from *Hebrew Melodies*, no. 18, published 1815

The Assyrians were the cruelest of any great nation of antiquity. King Asshurizirpal, commencing his reign in 883 BCE, penned this of his defeated foes: "Their men, young and old, I took as prisoners. Of some I cut off the feet and hands; of others I cut off the noses, ears, and lips; of the young men's ears I made a heap; of the old men's heads I built a minaret."[164]

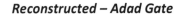

Reconstructed – Adad Gate

The Assyrians were ruthless in ravaging the homes and lives of the people they conquered, and gluttonous with the spoils of war. The city of Nineveh was evil personified; ripe for the wrath of a holy God.

At the same time in history, the Hebrews had grown decadent and perverse. Their land was divided into the northern kingdom of Israel and the southern kingdom of Judah; often warring with each other. Both partook in the sins of adultery, drunkenness, and idolatry. *Ba'al* worship was rampant. King Jeroboam of Israel reinstituted worship of the golden calves[165] while King Ahaz of Judah offered up his son in child sacrifice.[166] God commissioned the prophets Amos and Hosea to call the covenant people to repentance, and He commissioned Jonah to call the Ninevites to repentance.

---

[164] Hawlinson, "*Five Great Monarchies*" vol. 2, p85
[165] 1 Kings 12:28-31
[166] 2 Kings 16:3

Whether through divine revelation or familiarity with the prophecies of his contemporaries, Jonah came to realize God's intention in commissioning him to Nineveh. Jonah later confided to God: *"...was not this my saying, when I was yet in my country? Therefore I fled before unto Tarshish: for I knew that thou art a gracious God, and merciful, slow to anger, and of great kindness, and repentest thee of the evil."*[167]

God always provides Himself a witness,[168] and God often utilizes one's enemy to impart judgment.[169] Jonah foresaw the stark reality that the barbaric Assyrians would become God's instrument in judging the kingdom of Israel. Jonah wanted no part of it, and was willing to die in order to spare his countrymen from the horrific fate.

Jonah, of course, was unsuccessful in altering God's plan as he ultimately succumbed to preaching in Nineveh. To Jonah's dismay, he was an overwhelming success. Nineveh's repentance served as a rebuke to a proud and self-righteous Israel who believed being God's people was theirs by birth-right. God shunned them by extending grace to their enemy -- the most vile nation on the face of the planet. The prophet Jeremiah would offer the Israelites their final warning, yet Israel refused to repent and so -- just as Jonah feared -- the Assyrians invaded Israel and carried off its people into captivity.[170]

---

[167] Jonah 4:2
[168] Acts 14:17
[169] See Judges 6
[170] 2 Kings 17

The *Scroll of Jeremiah* reveals God's mercy towards Nineveh is an eternal spiritual principle, and wasn't preferential treatment intended to spite Israel:

> *At one moment I might speak concerning a nation or concerning a kingdom to uproot, to pull down, or to destroy it; if that nation against which I have spoken turns from its evil, I will relent concerning the calamity I planned to bring on it. (Jeremiah 18:7-8)*

Israel was unwilling to repent, so God was unwilling to relent. It's a time-tested principle that applies to Hebrew and Gentile nations alike; and it's a principle just as applicable today as it was in the days of Jonah and Jeremiah.

Consequently, about 150 years after Jonah, the prophet Nahum was dispatched to Nineveh to again warn its citizenry of the need to repent as had their forefathers. Nahum prophesized their destruction would include an *"overflowing flood;"*[171] perhaps intended to further malign their fish-god. That generation failed to heed the warning, and as a result its destruction came to pass in 612 BCE. Excavations have since confirmed, in part, flooding did indeed occur.

A continuing point of contention in regards to the *Scroll of Jonah* is that it's void of prophecy. However, just as there's prophetic imagery of Messiah upon the execution-stake found

---

[171] Nahum 1:8

in the *Scroll of Psalms*, so there's prophetic imagery of Jonah in the belly of the great fish in the *Scroll of Psalms*:

> *Thou hast laid me in the lowest pit, in darkness, in the deeps. (Psalm 88:6)*

> *… all thy waves and thy billows are gone over me. (Psalm 42:7b)*

> *Save me, O God; for the waters are come in unto [my] soul. (Psalm 69:1)*

> *…Thou hast kept me alive, that I should not go down to the pit. (Psalm 30:3b)*

> *In my distress I called upon the LORD, and cried unto my God: He heard my voice out of His temple, and my cry came before Him, [even] into His ears. (Psalm 18:6)*

> *I will pay my vows unto the LORD now in the presence of all His people. (Psalm 116:18)*

> *Restore unto me the joy of thy salvation; and uphold me [with thy] free spirit. [Then] will I teach transgressors thy ways; and sinners shall be converted unto thee. (Psalms 51:12-13)*

Even more compelling, amid Jonah's historical narrative, there's prophetic allegorical application. Jonah can be seen as a type of Israel, his flight conveys Israel's failure to fulfill its commission as a light to the nations, and the great fish is emblematic of Assyria/Babylon swallowing up Israel into captivity. Hosea 8:8 foretells *"Israel is swallowed up: now shall they be among the Gentiles..."* Jeremiah 51:34 foretells Babylon *"swallowed"* Israel *"like a dragon [or sea monster],"* and it *"filled his belly."*

The 'sea' is a metaphor for *the nations,* i.e. the Gentiles.[172] Therefore, Jonah in the belly of the great fish is indicative of Israel in the sea of nations -- the Diaspora. Jonah being swallowed but not digested represents Israel being among the Gentiles but not assimilated. The great fish vomiting Jonah out upon dry ground represents Israel being expelled from the nations and restored to the Promised Land.

As extrapolated from this allegory, it's noteworthy that Nineveh bordered on the Tigris River which doesn't empty into the Mediterranean Sea. Therefore, it's doubtful Jonah was vomited out upon the river-banks at the doorsteps of Nineveh. It's more likely Jonah was deposited back along the coastline of Israel from where he had to venture out -- as Israel is commissioned to do -- in order to share the Word of God with the Assyrians.

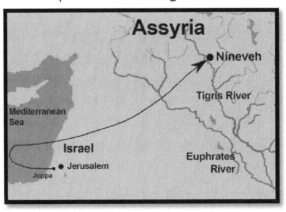

---

[172] See also Isaiah 60:5, Daniel 7:2-3, 7:17, and Revelation 13:1, 21:1.

When Jonah emerged from the great fish, his skin was severely burned from basking 72-hours in its gastric juices.[173] His pigmentation was completely gone, and likely all the hair on his body was eaten away. So while Jonah didn't stumble into Nineveh with seaweed still dangling about him, his marred appearance aided in convicting the hearts and minds of the citizenry. Luke 11:30 conveys *"...Jonah was a sign unto the Ninevites."*

Consequently, another facet Jonah had in common with Jesus was altered physical appearance. The lingering effects of Jonah's condition left him highly susceptible to the hot sun and wind. Jonah found some relief when God prepared a *gourd* [castor-bean plant] to protect and shelter him, and he was exceedingly glad.

This gourd which God prepared and for which Jonah *"hast not laboured, neither madest it grow..."*[174] is an allusion to the Promised Land for which the Hebrews neither labored nor planted:

> *And I have given you a land for which ye did not labour, and cities which ye built not, and ye dwell in them; of the vineyards and oliveyards which ye planted not do ye eat. (Joshua 24:13)*

---

[173] In the April 4, 1896, issue of *Literary Digest,* it relayed a story of a Mediterranean whale demolishing a harpoon boat. Two men were lost, but one was found alive in the whale's belly a day and one-half after It was killed. James Bartley lived with no ill effects, except that his skin was tanned by the gastric juices. (*Drake Annotated Reference Bible* – Matthew 12:40)
[174] Jonah 4:10

Alas, Jonah's protection didn't last long as the next morning God sent a worm to smote the gourd and cause it to wither. Therefore, just as Jonah found temporary relief in the gourd before it withered, post-exile Israel would find temporarily reprieve in the Promised Land before being banished.

Jonah's 'second calling' signifies the renewed opportunities for faith and obedience to the Law (of God by the hand of Moses) extended to post-exile generations. The 'east wind' that came up after the gourd withered is representative of judgment; as wind facilitates the separation of the wheat from the chaff.

> In that time it will be said to this people and to Jerusalem, "A scorching wind from the bare heights in the wilderness in the direction of the daughter of My people -- not to winnow and not to cleanse, a wind too strong for this -- will come at My command; now I will also pronounce judgments against them." (Jeremiah 4:11-12)

Jonah's enduring bitterness corresponds to the Hebrews' anger towards God for extending grace to the Gentiles rather than destroying them. This sentiment is later seen when the apostle Paul presented his defense before an assembly in Jerusalem. Everyone was captivated until Paul proclaimed that God had instructed him to *"Depart: for I will send thee far hence unto the Gentiles."*[175] Upon hearing those words, the crowd turned on Paul and began calling for his death.[176]

---

[175] Acts 22:21
[176] Acts 22:22

To state Jonah was an unwilling participant in his prophetic destiny is an understatement. Yet God was unwilling to let Jonah's defiance interfere with His desire to save the Ninevites, just as in Jesus' time God was unwilling to let Israel hinder His plan to extend salvation to the Gentiles:

> ...they [Hebrews] please not God, and are contrary to all men: Forbidding us to speak to the Gentiles that they might be saved, [and in so doing] fill up their sins alway: for the wrath is come upon them to the uttermost.
> (1 Thessalonians 2:15-16)

Further demonstrating Jonah as being a type of Israel is the numerous references to Jonah *descending* while the mariners are depicted as *ascending*. This is symptomatic of a warning in the *Scroll of Deuteronomy* wherein God imparts the consequences to Israel should they fail to obey His commandments:

> The stranger that is within thee shall get up above thee very high; and thou shalt come down very low. (Deuteronomy 28:43)

Jonah is described as going *"down to Joppa," "down into the sides of the ship," "he lay [down]," "the lot fell upon Jonah," "into the deep," "down to the bottoms of the mountains,"* etc. At the same time, the mariners arose up and came to know and worship the God of Abraham, Isaac, and Jacob.

As Jonah disobeyed God, so Israel was disobedient to God. The apostle Paul declared, *"But to Israel He saith, 'All day long I have stretched forth My hands unto a disobedient and gainsaying people.'"*[177]

Yet make no mistake -- God is not done with Israel. Just as God did not abandon Jonah, God will not abandon Israel. There are as-of-yet unfulfilled prophecies concerning Israelites who are to be gathered from among the nations and re-established in the Promised Land. Don't be deceived by the current nation-state of Israel; for the re-gathering of the house of Israel did not fully come to pass in 1948 CE by declaration of the United Nations. God will share His glory with no man.[178] Israel's re-gathering in the land promised to Abraham will be a miracle by the hand of the Almighty who alone will take the glory:

> *"Therefore, behold, the days come," saith* the
> LORD, *"that they shall no more say, 'The* LORD
> *liveth, which brought up the children of Israel
> out of the land of Egypt;' but, 'The* LORD *liveth,
> which brought up and which led the seed of the
> house of Israel out of the north country, and
> from all countries whither I had driven them;
> and they shall dwell in their own land.'"*
> (Jeremiah 23:7-8)

---

[177] Romans 10:21
[178] Isaiah 42:8

Clearly, this event hasn't yet happened, nor do people share this sentiment. But more profound, in the course of fulfilling Israel's destiny, the *Scroll of Ezekiel* foretells of a valley wherein a great number of Hebrews have been reduced to dry bones, but suddenly their bones begin to re-assemble, flesh and skin are added, the breath of life returns, and the multitude arises to their feet:[179]

> Then [God] said unto me, "Son of man, these bones are the whole house of Israel: behold, they say, 'Our bones are dried, and our hope is lost: we are cut off for our parts.' Therefore prophesy and say unto them, 'Thus saith the LORD GOD; "Behold, O My people, I will open your graves, and cause you to come up out of your grave, and bring you into the land of Israel."'" (Ezekiel 37:11-12)

Indeed, the day is still to come when the whole of Israel including generations past will inhabit the Promised Land whereupon they'll acknowledge Jesus as their Savior, their bitterness towards the Gentiles will be gone, and His millennial kingdom will extend over the entire earth as swords are beaten into plowshares[180] and mankind dwells in true peace.

The account of Jonah allegorically foretold the plight of the Hebrew people from the 8th century BCE through the 21st century CE, and allegorically foretells their future plight

---

[179] Ezekiel 37:1-10
[180] Isaiah 2:4

into the Sabbath millennium when Messiah will reign upon the Throne of David. This little scroll of seemingly abstract significance is in actuality a brilliant literary resource demonstrating an orchestrator of human affairs who is intimately aware of Israel's destiny.

The study of Jonah as a type of Israel is captivating, but Jonah can also be studied as a type of *disciple*. The journey from disobedience to obedience is one every disciple will take. In similar fashion, each must be immersed into the water and re-emerge with renewed dedication toward fulfilling God's commission.

Jesus made the association between *the belly of the great fish* and *the heart of the earth* when offering the *sign of Jonah*, and the two abodes are now synonymous. Scripture makes clear that all of mankind will enter the abode of the dead and be raised back to life whereupon they'll be judged:

> And as it is appointed unto men once to die, but
> after this the judgment... (Hebrews 9:27)

In this, too, Jonah is a shadow-picture of the disciples who shall be resurrected *"at the last trump."* Recall that when Jonah emerged from the great fish, his skin was without pigment and he was essentially bleached white. This is symbolic of purity and righteousness, and is representative of those who *"washed their robes, and made them white in the blood of the lamb."*[181]

---

[181] Revelation 7:14; see also Revelation 19:11

Just as Jonah was made white and vomited forth from the great fish, so those made white in the blood of the lamb shall be vomited forth from the earth to meet Jesus in the air:

> *Behold, I shew you a mystery; We shall not all sleep, but we shall all be changed, in a moment, in the twinkling of an eye, <u>at the last trump</u>: for the trumpet shall sound, and the dead shall be raised incorruptible, and we shall be changed. For this corruptible must put on incorruption, and this mortal must put on immortality.*
> *(1 Corinthians 15:51-53, emphasis added)*

> *For the Lord Himself shall descend from heaven with a shout, with the voice of the archangel, and <u>with the trump of God</u>: and the dead in [Messiah] shall rise first: Then we which are alive and remain shall be caught up together with them in the clouds, to meet the Lord in the air: and so shall we ever be with the Lord.*
> *(1 Thessalonians 4:16-17, emphasis added)*

Transitioning from Messiah's Second Coming at back of the Book to the creation account in the front of the Book, the *Scroll of Genesis* says God Almighty created mankind from the dust of the ground.[182] The name of the first man, *Adam* [אָדָם or *'adam* (Strong's #H120)], is a derivative of the word 'ground' [אדמה or *'adamah* (Strong's #H127)]. So it's intriguing that

---

[182] Genesis 2:7, 3:19

just as Jonah (whose name means 'dove') indwelt the great fish, so the Holy Spirit (symbolized by the dove) indwells men created from the ground.

This makes it all the more curious that early assemblies of men indwelt with the Holy Spirit used the symbol of the fish to identify one another!

Even today, the fish is a popular emblem, especially on cars, identifying someone as a disciple of Messiah. Yet in seeing it, most people envision Jesus' call to be *"fishers of men."*[183] In so doing, they miss the bigger picture right in front of their eyes: the great fish, the abode of the dead, the heart of the earth, three days and three nights, the *sign of Jonah*!

It's all so astounding. The depth of meaning within the *Scroll of Jonah* is surpassed only by the depths Jonah descended while in the belly of the great fish. In terms of Messianic typology with the *Scroll of Jonah*, three days and three nights barely scratched the surface (see Chapter Nine).

---

[183] Matthew 4:19; Mark 1:17

Chapter Six
Year of Messiah's Crucifixion

It is the glory of God to conceal a thing,
but the honour of kings is to search out a matter.
(Proverbs 25:2)

Evidences Dating the Crucifixion

M essiah's 72-hour entombment -- Wednesday evening through Saturday evening -- is further substantiated through historical means by demonstrating that Passover, in the year of Jesus' crucifixion, occurred on Wednesday. The problem is there's contention as to which year the crucifixion actually occurred. There's no consensus as to when Jesus was born -- most historians believe between 2- and 6 BCE, and there's no consensus on the duration of His ministry -- most theologians believe between 13 months and 3½ years.

The generally accepted year of Jesus' crucifixion is 33 CE due to Passover in that year occurring on Friday. Yet this belief is based upon two assumptions: 1) Jesus was 33 years of age when He was crucified, and 2) He was born just prior to 1 CE.

Ascertaining the truth is often times a battlefield of human tradition whereupon Scripture can be tortured to confess to any presupposition. In striving for objectivity, this inquiry aims to be liberally inclusive of many contending viewpoints.

The ultimate authentication of the year of Jesus' death would be the historical record of the Temple's veil ripping from top to bottom.[184] Although its occurrence is mentioned in the writings of *Josephus* and *Tacitus* as well as in the *Talmud*, none convey a means to date the event.

As a result, the starting point is John the Immerser who proclaimed the coming Messiah for only a short time before Jesus appeared on-scene.[185] The *Gospel of Luke* indicates John began immersing after the Word of God came to him in the wilderness.[186] Therefore, determining when the Word of God came to John will also determine, approximately, when Jesus began His public ministry.

The *Gospel of Luke* also provides the criteria by which to formulate a range of years as when Word of God came to John:

> *Pontius Pilate being governor of Judea [26 – 36 CE],[187] and Herod being tetrarch of Galilee [4 BCE – 39 CE],[188] and his brother Philip tetrarch of Ituraea and of the region of Trachonitis [4 BCE - 34 CE],[189] Lysanias the tetrarch of Abilene [unknown], Annas and*

---

[184] Matthew 27:51; Mark 15:38; Luke 23:45

[185] Mark 1:6-9

[186] Luke 3:2

[187] "Pontius Pilate" - *Encyclopedia Britannica,* 2004. Premium Service. http://www.britannica.com/eb/article?eu=61523

[188] "Herod Antipas" - *Wikipedia,* 2004. http://en.wikipedia.org/wiki/Herod_Antipas

[189] "Philip" - *Jewish Encyclopedia,* 2004. http://www.JewishEncyclopedia.com/view.jsp?artid=260&letter=P

Caiaphas being the high priests [18 – 36 CE],[190]
[when] the Word of God came unto John the son
of Zacharias in the wilderness. (Luke 3:1-2)

The corresponding dates relay a nine year range (26- to 34 CE) as to when the Word of God came to John whereupon he began immersing in the regions around the Jordan River.[191]

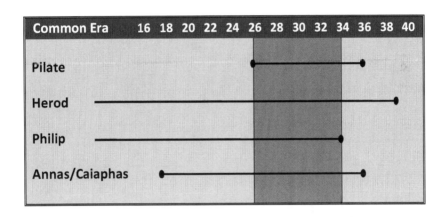

Reign of Caesar Tiberius

The *Gospel of Luke* further stipulates, *"Now in the fifteenth year of the reign of Caesar Tiberius... the Word of God came unto John."[192]* Caesar Tiberius served as co-regent with Caesar Augustus from 11- to 14 CE, but his capacities were limited. "From the beginning of 11 [CE], when he celebrated a magnificent triumph, to the time of the emperor's death in

---

[190] "Annas." *Jewish Encyclopedia,* 2004.
http://www.JewishEncyclopedia.com/view.jsp?artid=1554&etter=A
[191] Matthew 3:1-12; Mark 1:4-5; Luke 3:3
[192] Luke 3:1-2, emphasis added

14 [CE], Tiberius remained almost entirely in Italy, and held rather the position of joint-emperor than that of expectant heir."[193] Nevertheless, the Roman Senate named Tiberius as emperor on September 17th, 14 CE.[194] Upon ascending to the throne, Tiberius retroactively calculated his reign from Caesar Augustus' death on August 19th, 14 CE.[195]

Although seemingly simple to calculate the fifteenth year of Caesar Tiberius' reign, difficulties arise from the fact there are several methods of reckoning that may be utilized. Each has its strong-points and advocates. The five most prevalent are considered:

1. The Julian Calendar Non-Accession Year: entails reckoning years from January 1st, and counting whatever portion of the year in which a ruler ascends as his first. In the case of Tiberius, August 19th through December 31st of 14 CE constitutes his first year of reign, and, calculating forward, 28 CE constitutes his fifteenth year of reign.

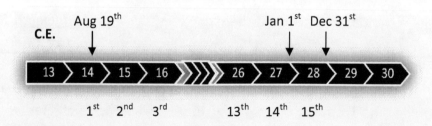

---

[193] *Encyclopedia Britannica* (Chicago: William Benton, Publisher, 1961), Vol. 22, p. 177.
[194] *Interpreters Dict. of the Bible*, Abingdon, 1962, Vol. 3, p. 640
[195] See Suetonius, Tiberius 73:1; Tacitus, Annals 1:5.

2. The Julian Calendar Accession Year: entails reckoning years from January 1st, but the remaining portion of the year in which a ruler ascends is an 'accession year' with his official reign beginning upon the New Year. This was the method used by Roman historians *Tacitus* and *Suetonius*. In the case of Tiberius, it means January 1st, 15 CE, commenced his first year of reign, and, calculating forward, 29 CE constitutes his fifteenth year of reign.

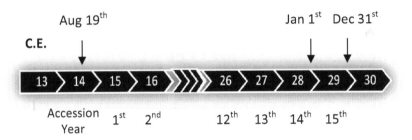

3. The Syro-Macedonian Calendar Non-Accession Year: entails reckoning years from the Macedonian New Year in late autumn, and counting whatever remaining portion of the year in which a ruler ascends as his first. This calendar was instituted by *Alexander the Great*, and was common through *Caesar Nerva* (96 – 98 CE). Adherents cite Luke being from Antioch and therefore employing the calendar with which he was first accustomed. Accordingly, August 19th through October 14th of 14 CE constitutes Tiberius' first year of reign and, less than two months later, October 15th commenced his second year of reign. Calculating forward,

September 21st, 27 CE, through October 8th, 28 CE, constitutes Tiberius' fifteenth year of reign.

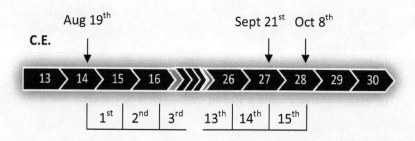

4. <u>The Syro-Macedonian Calendar Accession Year</u>: entails reckoning years from the Macedonian New Year in late autumn, but the remaining portion of the year in which a ruler ascends is an 'accession year' with his official reign beginning upon the New Year. Accordingly, August 19th through October 14th of 14 CE constitutes Tiberius' accession year, and October 15th commenced his first year of reign. Calculating forward, October 9th, 28 CE, through September 27th, 29 CE, constitutes Tiberius' fifteenth year of reign.

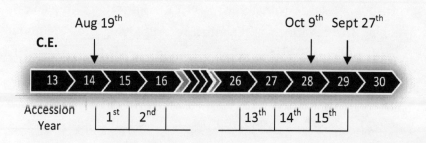

5. The Dynastic Year: entails reckoning years annually from the date of accession. This was the normal Roman method of reckoning,[196] and Luke seemingly addresses his accounts to a Roman official.[197] Accordingly, August 19th, 14 CE, through August 18th, 15 CE, constitutes Tiberius' first year of reign, and, calculating forward, August 19th, 28 CE, through August 18th, 29 CE, constitutes his fifteenth year of reign.

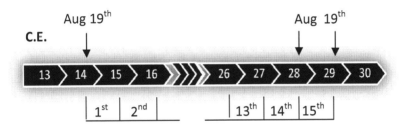

Therefore, in determining when the Word of God came to John the Baptist, the *Syro-Macedonian Calendar Non-Accession Year* serves as the earliest limiting point in time while the *Julian Calendar Accession Year* serves as the latest limiting point in time. In other words, *"the Word of God came unto John"* in September of 27 CE at the earliest, and December of 29 CE at the latest.

The next variant to be incorporated is the duration of time between the Word of God coming to John, and Jesus being baptized in the Jordan River. Logic dictates six months which

---

[196] Lewin, Thomas - *A Key to the Chronology of the New Testament* (London, 1865), p. 1iii
[197] Luke 1:1; Acts 1:1

correlates to the span of time between John's thirtieth birthday and Jesus' thirtieth birthday[198] (the age when a priest becomes able to serve[199]); however, to be safe, a full year will be allotted. Thus, Jesus was baptized between October of 27 CE and December of 30 CE.

From this window of starting dates, the potential durations of Messiah's ministry must be added in order to derive a range of years for His crucifixion. Utilizing the earliest possible date (October of 27 CE) and the shortest ministry term (13 months), the crucifixion necessarily culminated on the Passover of 29 CE. Since most scholars recognize 34 CE as the upper-most parameter for Messiah's crucifixion, there's no need to cap the maximum duration of His ministry given it terminates no later than Passover of 34 CE. This equates to a six year range (29- through 34 CE) for the year in which Messiah was crucified.

Dating Historic Passovers

The next step is to determine in which of these six years that Passover occurred on Wednesday. *Talmudic Judaism* utilizes a calendar formula wherein leap-months are systematically added 7 times amid a 19-year cycle. This affords very precise calculations for Passover both forwards into the future and backwards into antiquity. After compensating for lunar-drift over the past two millennia, this system insinuates Passover historically occurred as follows:

---

[198] Luke 3:23
[199] Numbers 4:3

Julian Calendar	
Year	Passover
29	Saturday, April 16
30	Wednesday, April 5
31	Monday, March 26
32	Monday, April 14
33	Friday, April 3
34	Monday, March 22

Passover occurred on Wednesday in the year 30 CE; and it appears to be the sole possibility. In fact, a large faction of Wednesday crucifixion advocates adheres to this 30 CE theory. But alarm-bells sound with the alleged need for human intervention in calibrating this calendar system for lunar-drift so as the calendar month correctly aligns with the New Moon.

In searching the Law (of God by the hand of Moses), it becomes apparent this calendar system isn't the one devised by the Almighty. To the contrary, this system was an invention of the Sanhedrin in 358/9 CE. In one of their last official capacities before being disbanded, this calendar was instituted so Jews in the Diaspora could uniformly observe high Holy Days from anywhere in the world.[200] With an inherent error less than that of the Julian calendar system, it served its intended purpose quite well; nevertheless, it still results in the New Year advancing on the equinox one day for every 216 years.[201]

---

[200] JewishEncyclopedia.com/articles/3920-calendar-history-of
[201] *Encyclopedia Britannica, s. v.* "Calendar," 9th ed., iv. 678

As for the matter at hand, this calendar is neither the Scriptural mandated reckoning nor the method used during the lifetime of Jesus. Therefore, it can't credibly be used in identifying the dates of Passover for the years in question.

Prior to 358/9 CE, the New Year was determined by two or three witnesses in the land of Judah observing the first sliver of the New Moon. Then, if the barley crop around Jerusalem was at a stage of ripeness (*abib*) ensuring its full maturity by the time of the First-fruits sheaf offering, the New Year was declared. Otherwise, if the barley wasn't *abib*, a thirteenth month (*Adar Bet*) was added and the New Year commenced upon the sighting of the next New Moon.

Unfortunately, there's no formula or methodology enabling a trustworthy reconstruction of all the elements needed to identify when the first sliver of the New Moon was historically sighted: the geometry of the sun and moon, the width and surface brightness of the lunar crescent, the scattering of the sun's light in the atmosphere, weather, and agricultural conditions. Therefore, conclusive dates for Passover cannot be readily identified, and any list purporting a specific date in any given year is somewhat disingenuous.

Nevertheless, honing a short-list of dates isn't rocket-science; and utilizing celestial software does prove advantageous. Software can historically simulate the geometric conditions of the sun and moon as they appeared over Judah for any given date under optimal circumstances.

Yet in implementing this data, it's important to distinguish between the scientific definition and the Biblical definition of 'New Moon.' The scientific definition pertains to the earth, moon, and sun being in conjunction with the dark side of the moon fully facing Earth; an unobservable mathematical moment in time. The Biblical definition pertains to the waxing crescent being first visible to observers in the land of Judah. As a result of refracting sunlight, the Biblical New Moon isn't visible to the naked-eye until shortly after sunset on the second or third day subsequent to the scientific New Moon. It then appears as a dim, thin sliver very low In the western horizon.

Scientifically, one lunar cycle is roughly 29.53 days. However, with the Biblical system being observation based, if the New Moon fails to be sighted in the evening of the thirtieth day (concluding a 29-day month), then the following evening is deemed the new month by default (resulting in a 30-day month).

Additionally, the New Year has a two month variant based upon the barley crop being *abib*. Together with two possible days in each month, this equates to four potential dates for Passover in any given year.

Remember, when determining dates for the sighting of the New Moon, days are reckoned from sunset to sunset. In effect, this means the Biblical date falls one day after the corresponding Julian calendar date.

Possible Passover	
Date	Day
Mar 19	Saturday
Mar 20	Sunday
Apr 17	Sunday
Apr 18	Monday
April 6	Thursday
April 7	Friday
May 6	Saturday
May 7	Sunday
March 26	Monday
March 27	Tuesday
April 25	Wednesday
April 26	Thursday

Possible Sightings of the New Moon in Judah				
Yr	Julian Date	Julian Day	Moon Visible	Hebrew Day
29 C.E.	March 5	Saturday	5:40 PM	Sunday
	March 6	Sunday	5:40 PM	Monday
	April 3	Sunday	5:57 PM	Monday
	April 4	Monday	5:58 PM	Tuesday
30 C.E.	March 23	Thursday	5:50 PM	Friday
	March 24	Friday	5:51 PM	Saturday
	April 22	Saturday	6:09 PM	Sunday
	April 23	Sunday	6:09 PM	Monday
31 C.E.	March 12	Monday	5:44 PM	Tuesday
	March 13	Tuesday	5:45 PM	Wednesday
	April 11	Wednesday	6:02 PM	Thursday
	April 12	Thursday	6:02 PM	Friday

↓

March 15	Saturday
March 16	Sunday
April 13	Sunday
April 14	Monday
April 3	Friday
April 4	Saturday
May 2	Saturday
May 3	Sunday
March 24	Wednesday
March 25	Thursday
April 22	Thursday
April 23	Friday

Year	Date	Time	Day	Day
32 C.E.	March 1	5:37 PM	Saturday	Sunday
	March 2	5:38 PM	Sunday	Monday
	March 30	5:56 PM	Sunday	Monday
	March 31	5:57 PM	Monday	Tuesday
33 C.E.	March 20	5:49 PM	Friday	Saturday
	March 21	5:50 PM	Saturday	Sunday
	April 18	6:06 PM	Saturday	Sunday
	April 19	6:07 PM	Sunday	Monday
34 C.E.	March 10	5:43 PM	Wednesday	Thursday
	March 11	5:43 PM	Thursday	Friday
	April 8	6:00 PM	Thursday	Friday
	April 9	6:01 PM	Friday	Saturday

Utilizing the astronomical chart on the previous pages, data relating to the years 29- through 34 CE reveals two potential dates for the Passover occurring on Wednesday.

Wednesday Passovers	
31 CE	34 CE
April 25	March 24

When integrating these dates for a Wednesday Passover with the 39-month window (October of 27 CE to December of 30 CE) for Jesus' baptism, the resultant ministry options are as follows:

> ➢ Jesus was baptized in October of 27 CE or shortly thereafter, allowing for a 3¼- to 3½ year ministry if crucified in 31 CE; and a 6¼- to 6½ year ministry if crucified in 34 CE.

> ➢ Jesus was baptized in 28 CE, allowing for a 2¼- to 3¼ year ministry if crucified in 31 CE; and a 5¼- to 6¼ year ministry if crucified in 34 CE.

> ➢ Jesus was baptized in 29 CE, allowing for a 16 month to 2¼ year ministry if crucified in 31 CE; and a 4¼- to 5¼ year ministry if crucified in 34 CE

> ➢ Jesus was baptized in 30 CE, allowing for a 13- to 16 month ministry if crucified in 31 CE; and a 3¼- to 4¼- year ministry if crucified in 34 CE.

The Temple Cleansing Incident

A dramatic incident occurred on Temple grounds during the first Passover following Jesus' baptism. It's documentation in the *Gospel of John* proves to be invaluable in dating the start of Jesus' ministry. After overturning tables and driving out the money-changers, John records a confrontation between Jesus and some Judeans (citizens of Judea) who sought a miraculous sign as authentication for His authority to do these things:

> Then answered the [Judeans] and said unto Him, "What sign shewest Thou unto us, seeing that Thou doest these things?" Jesus answered and said unto them, "Destroy this Temple, and in three days I will raise it up." Then said the [Judeans], "Forty and six years was this Temple in building, and wilt Thou rear it up in three days?" (John 2:18 – 20)

Jesus, of course, was referring to the Temple of His body,[202] but 46 years is the essential information gained from this exchange. It's an important reference point when in context of the Temple's refurbishment at the direction of Herod the Great.

Herod Antipas (Herod the Great) was founder of the Herodian dynasty which ruled over Judah from 37 BCE until its revolt against Rome in 66 – 70 CE. Herod was an *Edomite*,

---

[202] John 18:21

a hereditary enemy of the Jews, whose family was forcibly converted to Judaism under the Hasmonean Maccabees of the 2nd century BCE.

Bestowed with the title "King of the Jews" by Marc Anthony, Herod commissioned the second Temple to be remodeled and enlarged. As for his reason, rabbis speculate, "It was built by a sinful king, and the building was intended by him as an atonement for having slain Israel's sages."[203] Others contend Herod's intentions weren't so noble. Being unrelated to family with claim to rule, many refused to acknowledge or respect his authority. They suggested the Temple was a means for Herod to ingratiate himself in the hearts and minds of his citizenry.

After commissioning the colossal project, ground-breaking began in 20- or 19 BCE.[204] Therefore, the forty-sixth year from 20 BCE (no year zero) is 26 CE, and from 19 BCE is 27 CE. The problem is that these dates precede Caesar Tiberius' fifteenth year of reign, and are too early for Jesus to have begun His earthly ministry.

The solution is found in the obscure fact there are two words in Greek which are translated into English as *'Temple.'* The first word, ἱερόν or *hieron* (Strong's #G2411), refers to the entire area encompassing the Temple known as the "Court of Gentiles." Yet within the Court of Gentiles was a raised terrace known as the "Court of Women" wherein only Hebrew men

---

[203] Talmud, *Numbers Rabbah* 4:14
[204] http://www.jewishencyclopedia.com/view.jsp?artid=123&letter=T&search=heros'd temple

and their wives could enter; within the Court of Women was another raised terrace known as the "Court of Israel" wherein only Hebrew men could enter; and within the Court of Israel was a pinnacle terrace known as the "Court of Priests" wherein only Levites could enter. The second word, ναός or *naos* (Strong's #G3485), refers specifically to this inner-Temple, or Sanctuary, that housed the Holy Place and Holy of Holies.

When Jesus overturned the tables of the money-changers on Temple grounds, ἱερόν is used.[205] However, during the encounter wherein Jesus challenged the Judeans to destroy this Temple and He'd raise it up in three days, ναός is used.[206] This conveys that Jesus never implied He'd raise the entire Temple complex, but solely the Sanctuary of the Holy Place and

---

[205] John 2:14-16; see also 5:14; 7:14, 28; 8:2, 20, 59; 10:53; 11:56; and 18:20
[206] John 2:20

Holy of Holies. The inherent shadow-picture is considerable: Jesus is the true Sanctuary, and He's exclusively where believers must go to enter into the holy presence of God.

Moreover, in specifying the difference in locations, it's possible the Judeans didn't immediately confront Jesus after He drove out the money-changers, but rather He proceeded deeper into the Temple complex. One could speculate that Jesus climbed the steps of the Court of Priests and stood in or near the Sanctuary by authority of the Melchizedek priesthood, accompanied by John the Revelator who was from a family of priests;[207] perhaps a relation of the High Priest.[208] Consider also that John, after Jesus' arrest, was able to enter the courtyard of the High Priest and then gain authorization for Peter to enter. Perhaps only John's Gospel relays the Judean confrontation because only he was first-hand witness to the verbal exchange within the exclusive area.

If indeed the confrontation wherein the Judeans asked Jesus, *"What sign shewest Thou unto us, seeing that Thou doest these [plural] things?"* transpired in the Court of Priests, then the Judeans weren't merely inquiring as to why He had overturned the tables, but also as to why He dared enter the Court of Priests when He wasn't a Levite?!

---

[207] Polycrates, in the second-century, writes, "John, who was both a witness and a teacher, who reclined on the bosom of the Lord, and, being a priest, wore the sacerdotal plate." (Eusebius, *Church History,* Book V, Ch. 24)
[208] Acts 4:6

Noteworthy is the fact this confrontation was with *"Judeans"* as opposed to Pharisees or Sadducees, which may insinuate His accusers were the Levite Priests themselves!

Whatever the case, knowing Jesus' statement pertained to raising the Sanctuary (ναός) as opposed to the Temple grounds as a whole, reference to 46 years takes on a new perspective. Flavius Josephus, the premiere first-century Jewish-Roman historian, records the Sanctuary was the first section of Herod's reconstruction project, and it was completed by the priests in one year and six months without interruption to the daily sacrifices.[209]

This is relevant because grammatically the *aorist passive*, οἰκοδομέω or *oikodomeō* (Strong's #G3618) -- to build, to erect a building -- is typically translated as a *constative aorist*; which is a verb expressing an action regardless of extent, progress, or duration. This would be correct if applicable to ongoing construction on Temple grounds (ἱερόν), but its applicability to the refurbished Sanctuary (ναός) indicates it ought to be rendered as a *perfective aorist*; which is a verb expressing an action as complete.

Additionally, such a rendering better relates to the *temporal dative*, ἐγείρω or *egeirō* (Strong's #G1453), in that the first stage of construction -- refurbishment of the Sanctuary -- had at that point existed in its completed state for 46 years.

---

[209] Josephus. Ant. XV. II. 6 S 421

Refurbishing the Sanctuary was a joyous undertaking, and its rededication was a milestone in Temple history. For the Judeans, particularly the Levites, referring to the celebrated event was an extension of national identity. Akin to one's age, years aren't reckoned from stages or trimesters, but from birth; meaning years weren't calculated from the start of construction, but from its completion. Thus, it's entirely sensible for the Judeans to have questioned Jesus as to how He intended to raise up in three days this Sanctuary which at that time had existed in its refurbished state for 46 years.

Several Bible translations true to this grammatical principle render this verse in such a manner whereas this reckoning is discernible even through some otherwise obscure verbiage:

1599 Geneva Bible --

> Then said the Jews, 'forty and six years was the Temple [Sanctuary] a building, and wilt Thou rear it up in three days?'

Darby Translation (DBY) --

> The Jews therefore said, 'Forty and six years was this temple [Sanctuary] building, and Thou wilt raise it up in three days?'

Young's Literal Translation (YLT) --

> The Jews, therefore, said, `Forty and six years was this Sanctuary building, and wilt Thou in three days raise it up?'

The implication is even more apparent when the *simple past* form of 'be' (i.e. was) is replaced with the *present perfect* form (i.e. has been). This is a fair and reasonable modification being the grammatical entity *indicative of first and third person past tense* does not exist in Greek, and its implementation is solely to facilitate an idea inherent in the source text which cannot be literally translated. It's purely a matter of context, and the verse could just as easily, if not preferably, be translated as follows:

> Then said the Judeans, "Forty and six years has
> been this Sanctuary building, and wilt Thou rear
> it up in three days?"

Finally, with this passage in its rightful context, the grand implication of John 2:18-20 is that the fully refurbished Sanctuary had existed as a completed entity for 46 years at the time of the Judeans' sarcastic response to Jesus!

In dating the verbal exchange, it's logistically unreasonable to presume the priests began construction during the fall-feasts or winter months. Spring is the optimal time to undertake new construction; work on Solomon's Temple commenced on *the second day of the second month* (April/May),[210] and work on Zurubbel's (Second) Temple likewise commenced in *the second month*.[211] There's certainly no pressing reason to presume Herod's refurbishment commenced at some less opportune time.

---

[210] 1 Kings 6:1, 37; 2 Chronicles 3:2
[211] Ezra 3:8-11

According to Josephus, the first phase of construction -- the Sanctuary -- began in 20- or 19 BCE, and took 18 months to complete. So from the Sanctuary's completion in the autumn of 19- or 18 BCE respectively, 46 years equates to the autumn of 28- and 29 CE respectively,[212] and the subsequent Passover when the Temple Cleansing Incident occurred was in the spring of 29- or 30 CE respectively.

This means that Jesus commenced His ministry sometime after the Passover of 28 CE yet before the Passover of 30 CE. As a result, when implementing the terminal dates of Passover in 31- and 34 CE, the ministry options are as follows:

➢ Jesus was baptized after Passover in 28 CE, allowing for a 2¼- to 3 year ministry if crucified in 31 CE; and a 5¼- to 6 year ministry if crucified in 34 CE.

➢ Jesus was baptized in 29 CE, allowing for a 16 month to 2¼ year ministry if crucified in 31 CE; and a 4¼- to 5¼ year ministry if crucified in 34 CE.

➢ Jesus was baptized prior to Passover in 30 CE, allowing for a 13- to 16 month ministry if crucified in 31 CE; and a 4- to 4¼- year ministry if crucified in 34 CE.

These ministry options are controversial in that Jesus' ministry proves to be either significantly longer or shorter than the customary 3½ years of Christian and Catholic lore.

---

[212] Rededication occurred soon after Caesar Augustus visited Syria.
Duane W. Roller, *The building program of Herod the Great*, University of California Press, 1998, pp 67-71.

Origin of the Three and One-half Year Ministry

The duration of Messiah's ministry is another area in which conventional wisdom is in error. A three and one-half year Messianic ministry is parroted throughout Christendom. Yet most people have never contemplated the theological association between a Friday crucifixion and a 3½-year ministry. They're inexplicably tied to one another. Like dominoes, the Good Friday crucifixion and the 3½-year ministry either stand or fall together.

The origin of the 3½-year ministry can be traced back to Roman Emperor Constantine (306 – 337 CE). Known as Constantine the Great, he successfully united 'church' and 'state' by making Christianity the official religion of the Roman Empire. As Caesar of Rome, he bore the title *Pontifex Maximus* (the *pontiff*); which equates to the head of the pagan priesthood. Upon declaring himself to be head of the Church, he assumed the title *Vicarius Christi*; or "Vicar of Christ." Incidentally, both these titles are still held by the papacy to this day.

Constantine essentially combined the claim to have spiritual power over heaven and hell with the temporal power to rule over the earth, and proclaimed himself to be "God upon earth." Thereafter, the paganism of Rome was repackaged with Christian names, titles, and doctrines to produce a unified state religion known as Roman Catholicism, or "Roman Universalism."

Alexander Hislop, in his highly acclaimed book, *The Two Babylons,* writes: "To conciliate the pagans to nominal Christianity, Rome, pursuing its usual policy, took measures to get the Christian and Pagan festivals amalgamated, and, by a complicated but skillful adjustment of the calendar, it was found no difficult matter, in general, to get Paganism and Christianity -- now far sunk in idolatry -- in this as in so many other things, to shake hands."[213]

A man known as Eusebius of Caesarea (c. 263 – 339)[214] was Emperor Constantine's biographer and historian. Part of his job entailed documenting Constantine as "God upon earth" and therein manipulating Scripture to make it appear to advocate Constantine's divine authority. In so doing, Eusebius laid the foundations for Replacement Theology (the Church replacing *Yisrael*), Dominion Theology (the Kingdom of *Elohim* in the here-and-now), and Preterist eschatology (all prophecy including the *Scroll of Revelation* being fulfilled as of 70 CE). Once in place, the road was paved for the so-called "Vicar of Christ" to begin his millennial rule from his throne in Rome.

Consequently, all subsequent popes have also presumed this authority: "It is evident that the popes can neither be bound nor unbound by any earthly power, nor even by that of the apostle Peter, if he should return upon the earth; since Constantine the Great has recognized that the

---

[213] Alexander Hislop, *The Two Babylons*, p. 105
[214] http://en.wikipedia.org/wiki/Eusebius_of_Caesarea

pontiffs held the place of God upon earth, their divinity not being able to be judged by any living man. We are, then, infallible, and whatever may be our acts, we are not accountable for them but to ourselves."
(Pope Nicholas I, c. 858-67)

Former statue of *Jupiter*, re-dedicated as *St. Peter*

The apostle Peter is prominently invoked in the above sentiment because, as the tale goes, he was the first pope; with "Christ" building the Church upon him, and he then passing on that authority in an unbroken succession of popes through Emperor Constantine and forthwith to this very day.

In the course of founding Preterist eschatology, Eusebius needed to reinterpret all Biblical prophecy in context of having been fulfilled as of the Temple's destruction in 70 CE. In the case of Daniel's 70-Weeks, Eusebius cleverly conjured up the 70th week by concocting Messiah's 3½-year ministry followed by another 3½-years inserted in the *Acts of the Apostles* between the outpouring of the Holy Spirit at Pentecost, and Peter supposedly handing over the "keys to the kingdom" to Roman Gentiles in Caesarea when visiting the home of Cornelius.[215]

---

[215] Acts 10:1 – 11:18

Upon the alleged completion of the 70th week, it's claimed the Almighty's everlasting covenant with Israel was nullified (thereafter referred to as "the Old Testament"), and the Roman Catholic Church assumed its full millennial authority to rule over the earth in place of Christ.

At its heart is the misinterpretation of Daniel 9:27 which states, "*...in the middle of the week he will put a stop to the sacrifice and grain offering.*" When applying this verse to Messiah in context of an alleged Friday crucifixion, it necessitates His ministry to have endured 3½-years; i.e. half of 7-years, or the middle of a prophetic week.[216]

However, knowing that Messiah was literally crucified "*in the middle of the week*" (Wednesday), the prophetic implication of Daniel 9:27 is fulfilled and His ministry's duration is irrelevant. Therefore, Christendom isn't bound to a 3½-year ministry which is otherwise unsupported in prophecy, typology, or New Covenant chronology.

Prior to the fourth-century, nobody advocated a 3½-year ministry. The Catholic Encyclopedia candidly acknowledges Eusebius as its progenitor.[217] Moreover, in the fifth-century, a Christian historian named *Socrates Scholasticus* asserted that Eusebius had been a pawn of Constantine who contrived history for the "praises of the Emperor" rather than to record an "accurate statement of facts."[218]

---

[216] Numbers 14:34 and Ezekiel 4:6.
[217] Eusebius, *Demonstratio Evangelica* (published before 311) VIII, 106, 8
[218] Socrates Scholasticus, *The Ecclesiastical History,* Book I: 1

> Thus, with Friday exposed as an erroneous interpretation of *"day before the Sabbath,"* the necessity for Eusebius' contrived 3½-year ministry vanishes. It's a theory devoid of Scriptural and historical foundation; and being founded upon faulty premise and sinister origin, a 3½-year ministry can join its Friday cohort in the trash-heap of tradition.

Feast of Tabernacles and Last Great Day

At this juncture, it's possible to ascertain the year of Messiah's crucifixion from the Scriptural record of the *Feast of Tabernacles* and the *Last Great Day* which came to pass in the autumn preceding His final Passover. The Gospel of John spends the better part of four chapters (7:2 – 10:21) detailing the events and encounters of these feast days.

The Feast of Tabernacles is the third of the three mandated annual pilgrimages to Jerusalem.[219] Similar to the Feast of Unleavened Bread, it's a seven-day festival beginning on the 15th day of the month of the seventh month *(Tishri)* -- a high Sabbath -- and extends through the 21st day of the month.[220] Throughout the festival, families tabernacle in booths (temporary dwellings) with roofs of palm branches, partly open to the sky, to commemorate God's providence during the 40 years they wandered in the Arabian Desert.[221]

---

[219] Exodus 23:14-17, 34:23; Leviticus 23:37-38
[220] Leviticus 23:33-41; Numbers 29:12-39; Deuteronomy 16:13-16
[221] Leviticus 23:42-43

Immediately following the seven-day Feast of Tabernacles is the year's final high Sabbath known as the Last Great Day, more formally known as 'Eighth Day of Solemn Assembly,' which occurs on the 22nd day of the seventh month.[222] The purpose or meaning of this high Sabbath isn't completely understood in Hebrew culture. Nevertheless, the fall-harvest is over, and these two festivals comprise eight days of extravagant celebration and rejoicing.

During the second Temple period, four immense menorah–candelabrums with wicks weaved from the priests' worn-out vestments and fueled by multiple liters of oil were erected in the Court of Women. The *Gemara* says they stood 75 feet high.[223] The light was so bright that every courtyard in Jerusalem, full of booths, was illuminated.[224]

---

[222] Leviticus 23:36
[223] *Talmud*, Gemara Sukkah 52b
[224] *Talmud*, Mishna Sukkah 5:2-3

The imagery of Israel's distinguished sages dancing and juggling may be amusing, but three times Scripture commands celebration in connection with this festival.[225] Rabbi Simon ben Gamaliel, under whom the apostle Paul studied, would juggle eight torches as well as perform a handstand on two fingers.[226]

The *Mishna* records, "Pious men and men of good deeds would dance around with lit torches in their hands, singing songs and praises, while the Levites played harps, lyres, cymbals, trumpets, and innumerable other instruments..."[227]

John the Revelator's account of the Feast of Tabernacles begins in chapter 7. Jesus goes up to Jerusalem secretly, and doesn't openly teach until mid-way through the festival.[228] The narrative then skips ahead to the climatic seventh and last day of the Feast of Tabernacles, which became known as the "Great Hosanna"[229] in reference to its pinnacle ceremony. This day is not to be confused with the Last Great Day which is still to follow, but this is the last and great day of Tabernacles; literally *"on the last day, the great, of the Festival."*[230]

On this final day of the Feast of Tabernacles, the last of 70 sacrifices were offered on behalf of the Gentile nations.[231]

---

[225] Leviticus 23:40; Deuteronomy 16:14. and 16:15
[226] Ross, Leslie Koppleman, *Celebrate! A Complete Jewish Holidays Handbook,* (Jason Aronson Inc. Northvale, New Jersey, 1994) p.214
[227] *Talmud,* Mishna Sukkah 5:4
[228] John 7:2-14
[229] Ganzfried, Rabbi Solomon, *Code of Jewish Law Vol, 3 Revised Edition* (Hebrew Publishing Co., New York, 1961) p. 106
[230] John 7:37
[231] Numbers 29:12-34; Sukkah 55b

The daily procession around the Alter while singing *Hosanna* and waving *lulavs*[232] on this day rounded the Alter seven times, being symbolic of Messiah's expected deliverance.

Furthermore, on this final day arose a water libation ceremony which showcased a priest playing a flute leading another priest with a golden flask to the Pool of Siloam. In accordance with Isaiah 12:3, *"Therefore with joy shall ye draw water from the wells of salvation,"* the priest filled the flask with the pool's water and then returned to the Temple. Upon passing through the Water Gate, he was greeted with a blast from a golden *shofar* (ram's horn). Finally, the water was poured out with the customary pouring of wine into a basin at the foot of the Altar of Sacrifice which erupted in a huge release of steam.

It was a dazzling ceremony of sight and sound; a spectacle of color and light amid stirring music and song which tantalized the senses, but failed to quench the thirst of the soul. It was in the midst of this joyous event among the 24 divisions of priests, *lulva*-waving, *shofar*-blasting, *Hallel*-singing,[233] and water-pouring that Jesus cried out:

> *If any man thirsts, let him come unto Me, and drink. He that believeth on Me, as the Scripture hath said, out of his belly shall flow rivers of living water! (John 7:37-38)*

---

[232] Branches of palm, myrtle, and willow bound together
[233] Psalms 113-118

The significance was clearly understood by those in attendance: *"Many of the people therefore, when they heard this saying, said, 'Of a truth this is the Prophet.' Others said, 'This is the Christ.'*[234]

The feast concluded with the Sanhedrin upset with Jesus' teachings and disturbance of the festivities. Each member then returned to his own house for the night[235] as opposed to continuing to tabernacle in booths; confirmation the last and greatest day of the Feast of Tabernacles had ended and the Last Great Day had begun.

In Messianic understanding, dwelling in booths is symbolic of this temporary life[236] with these mortal bodies being the true booths[237] until Messiah's return whereupon believers will be changed in the twinkling of an eye.[238] The Feast of Tabernacles is a shadow-picture of the millennial reign of Messiah,[239] and the Last Great Day -- the final high Sabbath -- is a shadow-picture of the Great White Throne Judgment.[240]

---

[234] John 7:40-41a

[235] John 7:44-53

[236] I Peter 1:17

[237] 2 Peter 1:14

[238] I Corinthians 15:50-51; Philippians 3:21; I John 3:2

[239] Revelation 20:4-6

[240] Revelation 20:11-15

Early the next morning on the Last Great Day, Jesus was again found teaching in the Temple court.[241] Judgment being the theme of the day, Pharisees brought a woman caught in the act of adultery to Him for condemnation. Jesus said, *"He that is without sin among you, let him first cast a stone at her."* At that, one by one, beginning with the eldest, they dropped their stones and walked away.[242]

Not long afterwards, Jesus was among the crowds in the Temple Treasury whereupon He became entangled in another dispute with Pharisees. Jesus exclaimed, *"Ye judge after the flesh; I judge no man. And yet if I judge, My judgment is true: for I am not alone, but I and the Father that sent Me."*[243] The dispute degenerates to the point where the Pharisees implied Jesus to be an illegitimate child.[244]

Jesus retorted, *"Your father Abraham rejoiced to see My day; and he saw it, and was glad."* The Pharisees responded sarcastically, *"Thou art not yet fifty years old, and hast Thou seen Abraham?"* Jesus replied, *"Verily, verily, I say unto you, before Abraham was, I AM"*; therein claiming to be the voice of the burning bush! The Judeans considered that blasphemy and picked up stones to throw at Him, but Jesus slipped away and departed the Temple grounds.[245]

---

[241] John 8:2
[242] John 8:3-11
[243] John 8:12-16
[244] John 8:41
[245] John 8:56-59

John's narrative of the Last Great Day continues in chapter 9:

> *¹And as Jesus passed by, He saw a man which was blind from his birth... ⁶He spat on the ground, and made clay of the spittle, and He anointed the eyes of the man with the clay, ⁷and said unto him, "Go, wash in the pool of Siloam. He went his way therefore, and washed, and came seeing... ¹⁴And it was the Sabbath day when Jesus made the clay, and opened his eyes.*

This is one of four miracles Jesus performed which Jews believe only the Messiah will be able to do.[246] *"Since the world began was it not heard that any man opened the eyes of one that was born blind."*[247] Yet in so doing, Jesus made a mockery of rabbinic law. First, He spit; a violation of the Sabbath according to the Talmud.[248] Second, He made mud; the Talmud states nothing is to be made on the Sabbath.[249] And third, He healed; another act the Talmud expressly forbids on the Sabbath.

So in the course of performing a miracle unheard of in the history of the world, Jesus at the same time showed contempt for the organized religious hierarchy which had assumed control of the nation and made the Commandments of God a snare and a burden.

---

[246] The other three being cleansing of lepers, casting out at demon of dumbness, and raising the dead.
[247] John 9:32
[248] *Talmud*, Mishna Shabbat
[249] *Talmud*, Mishna Shabbat 7:2 and 24:3

Jesus again made reference to judgment in 9:39, but the sought-after information is found in 9:14, *"And it was the Sabbath day when Jesus made the clay, and opened his eyes."* Note that John the Revelator labeled the Sabbath following Passover as being a 'high day,' but here solely labels it as being the Sabbath. This stems from a cultural reckoning wherein the weekly Sabbath is the second holiest convocation of the year; the Day of Atonement being the holiest.[250] When an annual and weekly Sabbaths coincide, the weekly Sabbath takes precedent. Therefore, because the Last Great Day occurred on Saturday, John's silence in regards to the high Sabbath is the norm being the weekly Sabbath is the weightier of the two.

In terms of dating Messiah's ministry, determining the year in which the Last Great Day occurred on Saturday will identify the subsequent Passover as the one when Jesus was crucified:

	New Moon		Tabernacles		L.G.D.	
Yr	**Date**	**Day**	**Dates**		**Date**	**Day**
30 CE	Sept 15	Fri	Sept 30 – Oct 6		Oct 7	Sat ←
	Sept 16	Sat	Oct 1 – Oct 7		Oct 8	Sun
	Oct 15	Sun	Oct 30 – Nov 5		Nov 6	Mon
	Oct 16	Mon	Oct 31 – Nov 6		Nov 7	Tues
33 CE	Sept 13	Sun	Sept 28 – Oct 4		Oct 5	Mon
	Sept 14	Mon	Sept 29 – Oct 5		Oct 6	Tues
	Oct 13	Tues	Oct 28 – Nov 3		Nov 4	Wed
	Oct 14	Wed	Oct 29 – Nov 4		Nov 5	Thurs

---

[250] Leviticus 23:26-32

The Last Great Day coincided with the weekly Sabbath on Saturday, October 7th, 30 CE. This indicates that Jesus was crucified, dead, and buried on Wednesday, April 25th, 31 CE! Jesus' corpse was placed in the tomb that evening at dusk, He remained in the heart of the earth for three days and three nights, and He took up His life again at dusk on Saturday, April 28th, 31!

So with this major component in place, the potential start dates and durations of Messiah's ministry are as follows:

➢ Jesus commenced His ministry after Passover in 28 CE with the Temple Cleansing Incident occurring in the days before Passover in 29 CE, allowing for a 2- to 3 year ministry culminating on Passover in 31 CE.

➢ Jesus commenced His ministry shortly before the Temple Cleansing Incident in the days before Passover in 29 CE, allowing for a 2- to 2¼ year ministry culminating on Passover in 31 CE.

➢ Jesus commenced His ministry after Passover in 29 CE with the Temple Cleansing Incident occurring in the days before Passover in 30 CE, allowing for a 1¼- to 2 year ministry culminating on Passover in 31 CE.

➢ Jesus commenced His ministry shortly before the Temple Cleansing Incident in the days before Passover in 30 CE, allowing for a 13- to 16 month ministry culminating on Passover in 31 CE.

Annual Atonement Sacrifices

At this point, it's evident that Messiah's purported 3½-year ministry is a heretical derivative of Preterist eschatology and its obligatory Friday crucifixion. In solidifying this relationship, pursuing the duration of Messiah's ministry proves advantageous in that it undermines both a 3½-year ministry and the Good Friday – Easter Sunday tradition.

While far from an exhaustive examination into the matter, one intriguing method of narrowing the time-frame of Messiah's ministry is extracted from the *Babylonian Talmud*. Without question, the *Talmud* does not carry the weight and authority of Scripture, but as a historical text its insight into this matter is worthwhile.

The Day of Atonement (*Yom Kippur*) is the fifth of the seven high Sabbaths, and as mentioned earlier it's the single most solemn day of the year. God commands its observance on the 10th day of the seventh month;[251] five days before the Feast of Tabernacles and twelve days before the Last Great Day. Modern-day Jewish observances include reading the *Scroll of Jonah* in its entirety on this day. Yet back in Temple times, this high Sabbath is when the annual atonement sacrifices were offered up to the Almighty. According to rabbinic tradition, after the High Priest completed the atonement sacrifices, any one of three signs would indicate they'd been accepted and atonement for the nation had been granted.[252]

---

[251] Leviticus 23:27-32; Number 29:7-22
[252] Babylonian Talmud, *Yoma* 39a

One sign entailed a piece of scarlet cloth tied between the horns of a bull which was sacrificed by the High Priest prior to his passing through the veil into the Holy of Holies.[253] If it later turned white, it indicated God had forgiven Israel's sins in accordance with Isaiah 1:18 -- "*Though your sins be as scarlet, they shall be as white as snow.*" In years when none of the signs appeared, the people were ashamed and mourned; for it indicated God had not accepted their atonement sacrifices.

Insight into the matter at hand is gained through the *Talmud's* record that no atonement sacrifice was accepted during the Temple's final 40 years. The number 40 signifies probation and testing, and 40 years is a recurring theme in Scripture; i.e. the duration Israel wandered in the wilderness, the length of both King David's and King Solomon's reign, etc. However, while no sacrifice was accepted during the Temple's final 40 years, every sacrifice was accepted during the Temple's first 40 years: "Our Rabbis taught that throughout the forty years that *Shim'on the Tzaddic* (Simeon the Righteous) served ... the scarlet cloth would become white. From then on it would sometimes become white and sometimes not... Throughout the last forty years before the Temple was destroyed... the scarlet cloth never turned white."[254]

The second Temple was destroyed on the 9th of *Av* (July/Aug) in 70 CE. Since the Day of Atonement occurs on the 10th of *Tishri* (Sept/Oct), the very last Levitical observance of the Day of Atonement occurred is 69 CE. While it's uncertain whether

---

[253] Leviticus 16
[254] Babylonian Talmud, *Yoma* 39a-39b

sacrifices were offered during the Roman siege from 66 to 70 CE, it has no bearing on the reckoning. During the final forty Day of Atonement observances with a Temple -- 30- through 69 CE -- no sacrifice was accepted.

This also indicates, by default, the final accepted atonement sacrifice occurred in the year 29 CE. Therefore, regarding the duration of Messiah's ministry, there's no theological rationale for one or two years of accepted sacrifices followed by a single year of a rejected sacrifice. This suggests Jesus commenced His ministry after the Day of Atonement in 29 CE when the last sacrifice was accepted, yet before Passover in 30 CE as later that year atonement sacrifices would be forevermore rejected.

This makes Messiah's ministry -- immersion to crucifixion -- a total of 13- to 19 months in duration.

The deeper implication is that it was upon Jesus' baptism, not His death, when the Levitical system of sacrifice was rendered obsolete. Note the new-found relevance of Luke 16:16 – *"The law and the prophets [were] until John."* When John baptized Jesus and declared Him to be *"the Lamb of God,"* the purpose of the Levitical priesthood (shadow-picture showing the shedding of innocent blood is required to atone for sin) was fulfilled and a staggering change in the heavenly realm happened right at that moment.

This correlates to the shadow-picture of Aaronic priests who started their service in the Tabernacle at 30-years of age.[255] In

---

[255] Numbers 4:35. 39, 43, 47

this same sense, Jesus started His service as High Priest after the order of Melchezidek upon His baptism in the Jordan River at 30-years of age; not upon His death and resurrection at 31-years of age.

This likewise adds insight to comments Jesus made to the Samaritan woman at Jacob's Well. Having just celebrated Passover in Jerusalem with His new disciples and then having spent time immersing in the Jordan River,[256] it was probably early June of 30 CE when He passed through Samaria while making His way north to the Galilee. Upon conversing with the woman at the well, Jesus says:

> Ye [Samaritans] worship ye know not what; we know what we worship: for salvation is of the Jews. But the hour cometh, and now is, when the true worshippers shall worship the Father in spirit and in truth: for the Father seeketh such to worship Him. (John 4:22-23, emphasis added)

What Jesus essentially said is that significant change had already occurred, although revelation of that change was still to come. It seems part of that change included God's manifest presence in the Sanctuary having permanently ceased; although it wouldn't be apparent until the Day of Atonement later that year as never again would an atonement sacrifice be accepted.

---

[256] John 4:1-3

Interestingly, the *Talmud* also bears record of the *lot* that indicated which goat was to be sacrificed on Day of Atonement thereafter failed to rise of its own accord in the priest's right hand,[257] the Temple's western light no longer continually burned on its own, and the Temple's doors ceased to open of themselves.[258] Though the Temple still stood and the Levites continued their priestly duties, the Levitical system had come to an end. The Levitical priesthood had been superseded by the *Melchezidek* priesthood.[259]

As a result of the change in priesthood and God thereupon vacating the Sanctuary, the unaccepted atonement sacrifices on the Day of Atonement surely confused many of Jesus' disciples; possibly even being interpreted as a divine rebuke of Jesus' ministry. After all, if the Messiah has come, shouldn't God be pleased?! The psychological ramifications of God seemingly being displeased tested the faith of some of the disciples, and because the Day of Atonement occurs only five days before the Feast of Tabernacles, the misperceived significance of the rejected atonement sacrifice may have played a part in many who thereafter disassociated themselves just prior to their pilgrimage up to Jerusalem.

> *From that [time] many of His disciples went back, and walked no more with Him... Now [God's] Feast of Tabernacles was at hand.*
> *(John 6:66, 7:2)*

---

[257] Babylonian Talmud, *Rosh Hashana* 31b
[258] Babylonian Talmud, *Yoma* 39b
[259] Psalms 110:1-4; Hebrews 5:6-10, 6:20, 7:1-21, 8:1

One Year Ministry Perspectives

The fact that Jesus' ministry was 13- to 19 months in duration runs contrary to popular theology, especially in light of the purported four Passovers in the *Gospel of John*:

1) the first in Jesus' ministry per 2:13-3:21
2) a *"Judean Festival"* encompassing chapter 5
3) mention of an approaching Passover in 6:4
   but for which nobody goes to Jerusalem nor observes
4) the Passover whereupon Jesus is crucified

First, to surmise the *"Judean Festival"* of chapter 5 to be Passover is overly presumptuous. It's never referred to as Passover, and to so allege relegates Messiah's first year of ministry to a mere chapter and one-half (John 3:22 – 4:54). In actuality, there are three Passover references in the *Gospel of John*. That advocates, at most, a 25- to 35 month ministry; not the 42 months needed to comprise 3½ years.

Second, when scrutinizing the alleged Passover of John 6:4, it's found to occur about the time of the feeding of 5000; likewise chronicled in all three synoptic Gospels without any suggestion of it being near the time of Passover.[260] Furthermore, the invoked emblem of bread in the feeding of 5000 is contrary to the symbolism associated with Passover when all leavened products are discarded.

---

[260] Matthew 14:13-21; Mark 6:30-44; Luke 9:10-17.

Making the ill-placed Passover of John 6:4 more suspect is its conspicuous absence from a thirteenth-century copy of the *Gospel of John* known as *Minuscule 472*.[261] Minus the ten words of verse 4 -- *"And the Passover, a feast of the Jews, was nigh"* -- the historic text states, *"And Jesus went up into a mountain, and there He sat with His disciples. When Jesus lifted up [His] eyes and saw a great company come unto Him, He saith unto Philip..."* (John 6:3 & 5) It reads flawless without the alleged Passover, and adds weight to the theory verse 4 was sinisterly added to corrupt the Gospel account.

Also conspicuous is the wording – *"a feast of the Jews"* – which smacks of anti-Semitic third-person analysis, and is an utterly implausible word choice from a Levite apostle.

Chronologically, when the Passover of verse 6:4 is absent, the *Gospel of John* clearly encompasses one year of cyclical feasts including Passover (ch. 2-3), Pentecost (ch. 5), Tabernacles (ch. 7), Last Great Day (ch. 8-9), Hanukkah (ch. 10-11), and Jesus' final Passover (ch. 12-20). From a design perspective, the Passover in John 6:4 wreaks havoc on an otherwise orderly accounting of God's annual Sabbaths and feasts.

Consider also that the Gospels of Matthew, Mark, and Luke all contend Jesus had a one-year ministry entailing only two Passovers: the first shortly after His baptism, and the second upon which He was crucified.

---

[261] *Minuscule 472* is a Greek minuscule manuscript of the New Testament currently housed at the Lambeth Palace (1177), London.

Moreover, a ministry of about one-year was the position of all early Church Fathers throughout the first three centuries. These include Irenaeus (c. 115(?) – 202) who wrote Jesus' ministry was "only one year and a few months;"[262] Clement of Alexandria (c. 150 – 215) who taught "it was necessary for Him to preach only a year;"[263] and Julius Africanus (c. 160 – 240) who said Jesus was 30-years of age when baptized and 31-years of age when crucified.[264]

Similar sentiments were shared by *Origen*,[265] *Tertullian, Ephraem, Gaudentius, Orosius,* and others amid the early centuries without dissention.[266] Even *Basilides*, a renowned Gnostic-preacher, taught Jesus had a one-year ministry.[267]

These early Church Fathers were not idiots incapable of understanding the implications of a third Passover in terms of ministry duration.

More recent advocates of a 1- to 1½ year ministry include von Soden,[268] Goguel,[269] Olmstead,[270] and Rood.[271]

---

[262] Ireneaus, *De Principiis* book iv, chapter 1, p. 5

[263] Clement of Alexandria, *Stromata,* book i. chapter 21.

[264] Julius Africanus, Chronicles, S.D.F Salmond, trans. Ante-Nicene Fathers, Vol. 6. Edinburgh: T & T Clark, 1980. Hbk. ISBN: 0567093794. pp.130-138.

[265] Origen, *De Principiis* book iv, chapter 2, p. 5

[266] Catholic Encyclopedia: Chronology of the Life of Jesus Christ, Relative Chronology, The public life of Jesus: its duration; newadvent.org/cathen/08377a.htm

[267] Clement of Alexandria, *Stromata,* book i. chapter 21, p. 146

[268] Hermann von Soden, "Chronology," *Encyclopaedia Biblica,* ed. by T. K. Cheyne and T. Sutherland Black, I (1899), pp. 802-3.

Be that as it may, Gospel chronology and early Church Fathers are not the only testimonies of Messiah's 13- to 19 month ministry. Once the blinders of preconception come off, many formerly obscure details emerge in radiant focus...

Male Yearling

Perhaps the most foundational application relative to the duration of Jesus' ministry is Exodus 12:5 which requires the Passover lamb to be a yearling; between one and two years of age -- *"Your lamb is to be a year old male without blemish."* As a shadow-picture pointing to Messiah's sacrificial death, it's fitting that Jesus' ministry lasted between one and two years starting with His baptism whereupon John the Baptist proclaimed, *"Behold, the Lamb of God, which taketh away the sin of the world."*[272]

A ministry between 13- and 19 months makes Jesus that male yearling without blemish at the time of His crucifixion. It's another captivating shadow-picture in the imagery of Jesus being, as the apostle Paul said, *"our Passover"*[273]

---

[269] Maurice Goguel, *The Life of Jesus*, trans. by Olive Wyon (London, 1933), pp. 233-52.
[270] A. T. Olmstead, "The Chronology of Jesus' Life," *Anglican Theological Review,* XXIV (January, 1942), 1-26, esp. 6-11; A.T. Olmstead, *Jesus in the Light of History* (New York, 1942), p. 281.
[271] Michael Rood, *The Chronological Gospels and Seventy Week Ministry of the Messiah* (Atlanta, 2013).
[272] John 1:29
[273] 1 Corinthians 5:7

Synagogue Reading

Jesus made an interesting assertion early in His ministry, recorded in the *Gospel of Luke*. Upon entering His hometown of Nazareth, Jesus was afforded the privilege of reciting the Sabbath's Scripture-reading in the synagogue.

And there was delivered unto Him the [Scroll] of the prophet [Isaiah]. And when He had opened the [scroll], He found the place where it was written:

The Spirit of the LORD is upon me, because he hath anointed me to preach the Gospel to the poor; he hath sent me to heal the brokenhearted, to preach deliverance to the captives, and recovering of sight to the blind, to set at liberty them that are bruised, <u>to preach the acceptable year of the LORD,</u>

And He closed the [scroll], and He gave it again to the [attendant], and sat down. The eyes of all them that were in the synagogue were fastened on Him. And He began to say unto them, "This day is this Scripture fulfilled in your ears."
(Luke 4:16-21, emphasis added)

Everyone's eyes remained upon Him because in reading the *Scroll of Isaiah*, He stopped and sat down without reading the full portion. Jesus terminated mid-sentence, essentially at a comma separating *"the acceptable year of the LORD"* from *"the day of vengeance of our God;"* a comma which has lasted about 2000 years.[274] Clearly, *"...the day of vengeance of our God"* is in reference to Messiah's Second Coming when He shall execute judgment upon all the earth; but *"the acceptable year of the LORD"* is in reference to Messiah's First Coming, and notably infers a singular year.

Epiphany and Timkat

Although a 3½-year ministry necessarily places Jesus' immersion in autumn opposite of His spring crucifixion, a ministry of 13- to 19 months vastly opens up the possibilities. In this context, it's interesting that Eastern Churches celebrate the festival of *Epiphany*, primarily commemorating Jesus' immersion, on January 6th.[275] Its observance traces back to at least the fourth-century when, on January 6th and 7th of 381 CE, St. Gregory of Nazianzus preached it as being the anniversary of Jesus' immersion.[276]

Similarly, Ethiopians to this day commemorate the festival of *Timkat* on January 19th with an elaborate celebration wherein replicas of the Arc of the Covenant are reverently wrapped and then borne in procession, carried upon the head of a

---

[274] See Isaiah 61:2

[275] It also commemorates Jesus' birth, the visit by the Magi, and the miracle at the wedding in Cana; though immersion is the primary reason. Cyril Martindale, *The Catholic Encyclopedia,* Vol. 5 (Robert Appleton Company, New York 1905), s.v., Epiphany.

[276] St. Gregory Nazianzus, *Orations xxxix* and *xl* P.G., loc. cit.

priest, to a nearby body of water. The ceremony is said to commemorate Jesus' manifestation as the Messiah arriving at the Jordan River to be immersed by John the Baptist.

Ethiopian priest carrying a replica of the Arc of the Covenant in a Timkat ceremony at Gondar, assisted by a deacon holding a liturgical parasol.

Presumably the Ethiopian eunuch immersed by Phillip relayed this information to Ethiopia's Queen Candace,[277] and it has since been passed down generation to generation.

Moreover, it's possible the 10-day variant between the two traditions is the result of Pope Gregory XIII's reform in 1582 CE when he subtracted ten days from the calendar.

Regardless of the factual basis of either tradition, the point is that these festivals demonstrate an early dissention from Messiah's baptism being in autumn. Both insinuate a ministry beginning in late winter: Jesus being baptized in mid-January, enduring forty days of fasting through February, then going to Jerusalem and selecting His initial disciples, returning to Galilee for *"not many days,"*[278] and finally venturing back to Jerusalem in early April for the Passover whereupon the Temple cleansing incident ensued.

---

[277] Acts 8:26-39
[278] John 2:12

Great Signs Upon Temple Grounds

Two extra-biblical sources record remarkable events on the Temple grounds during the eighth night in the month of the *Abib* in 30 CE; the eighth night into *"the acceptable year of the* LORD.*"* Again, while not Scripture, they provide fascinating historical insight.

As documented in the *Talmud*: "Forty years before the Temple was destroyed [in 70 CE] ... the gates of the *Hekel* [Holy Place] opened by themselves, until Rabbi Yohanan B. Zakkai rebuked them saying, '*Hekel, Hekel,* why alarmist thou us? We know that thou art destined to be destroyed...'"[279]

Josephus, the first-century Jewish-Roman historian, elaborates on these happenings: "Thus also, before the Jewish rebellion [66 – 70 CE], and before those commotions which preceded the war, when the people were come in great crowds to the feast of Unleavened Bread, on the eighth day of the month *Xanthicus* [*Abib*] and at the ninth hour of the night [3 A.M.], so great a light shone round the Altar and the holy house that it appeared to be bright day-time; which light lasted for half an hour.

"This light seemed to be a good sign to the unskillful, but was so interpreted by the sacred scribes as to portend those events that followed immediately upon it. At the same festival also, a heifer, as she was being led by the High Priest

---

[279] Talmud, *Yoma* 39b

to be sacrificed, brought forth a lamb in the midst of the Temple. Moreover, the eastern gate of the inner [court], which was of brass, and vastly heavy, and had been with difficulty shut by twenty men, and rested upon a basis armed with iron, and had bolts fastened very deep into the firm floor which was there made of one entire stone, was seen to be opened of its own accord about the sixth hour of the night.

"Now, those that kept watch in the Temple came thereupon running to the captain of the Temple, and told him of it; who then came up thither, and not without great difficulty was able to shut the gate again. This also appeared to the vulgar to be a very happy prodigy, as if God did thereby open them the gate of happiness. But the men of learning understood it, that the security of their holy house was dissolved of its own accord, and that the gate was opened for the advantage of their enemies. So these publicly declared that this signal foreshewed the desolation that was coming..."[280]

It's a stunning episode in Jewish history made all the more compelling because of its timing amid the start of Jesus' ministry. Just two days later Jesus was cleansing the Temple grounds of money-changers in the forty-sixth year of the refurbished Sanctuary. Six months later, the first of the final forty Atonement sacrifices was rejected. It all aligns perfectly with *"the acceptable year of the LORD"* being 30 CE; one year before the yearling Passover Lamb of God was sacrificed on Wednesday, April 25th, 31 CE.

---

[280] Josephus, *Wars of the Jews* (IV,5,3)

Josephus' Other Historical Insights

As discussed at the start of the chapter, the Gospel of Luke records it was during Caesar Tiberius' the fifteenth year of reign when the Word of God came to John the Baptist. Knowing Jesus died upon the Passover of 31 CE, a Messianic ministry of 13- to 19 months indicates the Word of God came to John in 29 CE. As a result, Luke's implemented calendar system is either the Julian Calendar Accession Year (Jan to Dec of 29 CE), the Syro-Macedonian Calendar Accession Year (Oct 28 CE to Oct 29 CE), or the Dynastic Year (Sept 19, 28 CE to Sept 18, 29 CE).

Further corroboration is found in Josephus' mention of Pontius Pilate being appointed as Roman *Prefect of Judaea* during Caesar Tiberius' twelfth year of reign.[281] Josephus indicates that Pilate held the position for 10 years until being deposed by *Lucius Vitellius*[282] shortly before his visit to Jerusalem just prior to Passover in 36 CE.[283] Consequently, Pilate's decade of service entailed the years 26 – 36 CE.

Knowing that Pilate's appointment as *Prefect of Judaea* transpired amid Tiberius' twelfth year of reign in 26 CE, it's thereby known that Tiberius' fifteenth year of reign occurred in 29 CE. This means that Roman/Jewish history is in harmony with Messiah's 13- to 19 month ministry, and that Josephus

---

[281] Schürer, *The History of the Jewish People in the Age of Jesus Christ*, T & T Clark, 1987, Vol. 1, p. 382, fn. 130.
[282] https://en.wikipedia.org/wiki/Lucius_Vitellius_the_Elder
[283] Josephus, *Antiquity of the Jews*, xviii, 4, 2

can be counted among the advocates of 29 CE being when the Word of God came to John.

Also resolved is the year in which Herod began the reconstruction and expansion of the Temple complex. The Temple Cleansing Incident occurred at Passover in 30 CE, which means the autumn of 29 CE marked the 46th year since the completion of the Sanctuary's refurbishment. Therefore, its completion occurred in the autumn of 17 BCE. With Josephus recording it took a year and one-half to do so, Herod's reconstruction project started in the spring of 19 BCE.

Summary of Messianic Ministry

29 C.E.

❖ Caesar Tiberius' fifteenth year of reign.

❖ The Word of God comes to John who begins baptizing throughout the region around the Jordan River.

❖ Jesus turns 30 years of age.

❖ After the Day of Atonement, in late 29 CE or early 30 CE, Jesus is baptized and commences a ministry of 13- to 19 months.

30 C.E.

❖ New Year commencing *"the acceptable year of the LORD"* likely begins on the evening of Friday, March 24th (otherwise on the evening of Thursday, March 23rd).

❖ The first Temple cleansing incident wherein Jesus claims He'll raise up the Sanctuary of His body in three days occurs during the week of April 2nd.

❖ Passover: the first in Jesus' ministry with His disciples likely occurs on Friday, April 7th (otherwise Thursday, April 6th).

❖ High Sabbath: the Feast of Unleavened Bread likely commences on Saturday, April 8th (or Friday, April 7th), and continues for seven days through Friday, April 14th (or Thursday, April 13th).

❖ Pentecost: the *"Judean festival"* of John 5 for which Jesus ventures up to Jerusalem; the year's third High Sabbath -- Sunday, June 4th.

❖ Day of Atonement: sacrifices are rejected as God has permanently vacated the Sanctuary -- likely Wednesday, Sept 27th (otherwise Tuesday, Sept 26th)

31 C.E.

❖ New Year begins on the evening of Wednesday, April 11th.

❖ Last Supper: Jesus institutes the New Covenant with its symbols of bread and wine in the upper-room with the twelve apostles -- Tuesday, April 24th.

❖ Passover: Jesus is arrested, tried, crucified, dead, and buried -- Wednesday, April 25th.

❖ High Sabbath: first day of the Feast of Unleavened Bread – chief priests approach Pilate, tomb is sealed and guards are posted -- Thursday, April 26th.

❖ Galilean women buy and prepare spices with which they intend to anoint His corpse -- Friday, April 27th.

❖ Weekly Sabbath: Jesus arises from the grave at evening -- Saturday, April 28th.

❖ The feast of First-fruits: Jesus appears to Mary of Magdalene, is accepted by God the Father as the sheaf-offering, and manifests to those gathered in the upper-room -- Sunday, April 29th.

Chapter Seven:
Prophetic Authentication

For the testimony of Jesus is the spirit of prophecy.
(Revelation 19:10)

Startling Fulfillments of Prophecy

In conclusively determining the day of the week when Messiah's crucifixion, death, and burial came to pass -- and thereby demonstrating He successfully fulfilled three days and three nights in the heart of the earth per the *sign of Jonah* -- authentication is achieved through multiple layers of corroboration: His personal testimony, the Gospel narratives, historic reference, Scripture typology, and prophecy. In delving into the prophecy aspect, the Triumphal Entry is a notable point of interest. While its supposed timing amid events leading up to the Passover shall likewise be relegated to tradition, prophecies hinging upon Messiah's Triumphal Entry prove to be the ultimate confirmation of His Wednesday crucifixion in the year 31 CE.

Summary of Triumphal Entry

In preparation for the Passover and the Feast of Unleavened Bread, the whole country is on the move. Jerusalem is bustling, the inns are full, and the money-changers are greatly profiting. Jesus' arrival is anticipated by believers and skeptics alike. Departing Bethany, Jesus ascends the Mount of Olives. Along the way, two disciples enter the village ahead and return with a donkey and its colt. The disciples then cast their outer garments upon the animals, Jesus mounts, and they descend along the road leading into Jerusalem.

As word spreads of Jesus' imminent arrival, the masses line the roadside. People cast their garments upon the ground while others cut branches from trees and likewise lay them before His path. The crowds proclaim, *"Hosanna to the son of David! Blessed is He that cometh in the name of God! Hosanna in the highest!"*[284] The Pharisees become upset with this seeming display of blasphemy, and admonish Jesus to quiet the crowds. Jesus responds, *"I tell you, if these should hold their peace, the stones would immediately cry out!"*[285]

---

[284] Matthew 21:9; Mark 11:9-10; and Luke 19:38
[285] Luke 19:40

The people's hearts yearn for Jesus to ride into Jerusalem and proclaim Himself to be king. They foresee the Romans expelled from the holy city, and Judah again established as a free and independent nation. Although they'd attempted several times over the past year to declare Him king, Jesus deliberately avoided it; that is, until this day when He meticulously arranges it. Riding a donkey in through the East Gate, Jesus deliberately fulfills the prophecy spoken of by Zechariah wherein Messiah presents Himself in this very way:

> *Rejoice greatly, O daughter of Zion; shout, O daughter of Jerusalem: behold, thy King cometh unto thee: he is just, and having salvation; lowly, and riding upon an ass, and upon a colt the foal of an ass. (Zechariah 9:9)*

Upon entering Jerusalem, the inhabitants note the commotion. They inquire who entered the holy city amid such fanfare, and His disciples make it known that He's *Yahshua ben Yosef*[286] of *Nazareth*. The procession continues onward to the Temple grounds where Jesus cleanses it of profiteers in the same manner He did the year before.[287]

In addition to the Triumphal Entry's literal occurrence, it proves key in both prophetic and typological aspects. Its timing is relevant to the shadow-picture of Jesus being the Passover Lamb of God, and constitutes an amazing fulfillment of Messianic prophecy as foretold in the *Scroll of Daniel*.

---

[286] Son of Joseph
[287] Mark 11:11

Palm Saturday

While tradition teaches the Triumphal Entry occurred on Sunday, the Levitical shadow-picture demonstrates this was not the case. The Passover lamb was to be selected on the 10th day of the first month. Therefore, with Jesus being the Passover Lamb of God, the Levitical command is a shadow-picture of the day when Israel would be presented with the Lamb that Abraham had promised God would provide:

> *Tell the whole community of Israel that on the tenth day of this month [in the Abib] each man is to take a lamb for his family ... Take care of them until the fourteenth day of the month, when all the people of the community of Israel must slaughter them at twilight. (Exodus 12:3-6)*

Jesus -- the Lamb of God -- is presented -- makes His triumphal entry -- on the 10th day of the first month. Then, as the Passover lamb is taken home and inspected for imperfection over the course of four days, Jesus appears in the Temple (House of God) over the course of four days whereupon Israel inspects Him for imperfection. Once the lamb is found to be without defect or blemish, it's slaughtered as the Passover sacrifice at evening on the 14th day of the month.

This incontrovertibly means the Triumphal Entry occurred four days prior to Passover rather than the traditional five days as is the case with a Sunday Triumphal Entry and Friday crucifixion.

Accordingly, when the 14th day of the month occurs on Wednesday, the 10th day occurs on Saturday!

ABIB 31 C.E.						
Sun	Mon	Tue	Wed	Thur	Fri	Sat
				1	2	3
4	5	6	7	8	9	10
11	12	13	14	15	16	17
18	19	20	21	22	23	24
25	26	27	28	29	30	

Had Passover occurred on Friday per the tradition, then the Triumphal Entry four days earlier would've fallen on Monday. Either way, Palm Sunday is a misnomer; a false teaching without foundation in the Hebrew Bible (Old Testament) or Messianic (New Covenant) writings.

The Triumphal Entry occurring on Saturday may raise questions about the Fourth Commandment's instruction to rest on the Sabbath, but the trek from Bethany to Jerusalem is short; within the arbitrary limits of the rabbinic *Sabbath's day journey*.[288] In fact, not only Jesus and His disciples, but all the Hebrew pilgrims celebrating the festivals routinely walked to Jerusalem from surrounding areas on each and every day of the feast including weekly- and high Sabbath days.

In regards to Jesus riding a donkey on the Sabbath, Scripture commands: "...*You are not to do any work, neither you, nor*

---

[288] Acts 1:12

your son, nor your daughter, nor your male or female servant, nor your livestock, nor the alien who is within your gates, because the LORD made the heavens and the earth and the sea, and all that is in them, in six days, then He rested on the seventh day..."[289] It's important to note Jesus' specific request for a colt, meaning it was still with its mother and hadn't yet been ridden or entered the workforce. As such, it wasn't subject to six days of work followed by a Sabbath rest. Therefore, in keeping with both the letter and spirit of Law, Jesus is blameless when entering Jerusalem upon the back of an untamed colt on Saturday.

It's also provocative that Hebrews historically refer to the Saturday before Passover as *Shabbat HaGadol,* meaning 'the Great Sabbath.'[290] According to Unger's Bible Dictionary: "the [Great] Sabbath immediately preceding the Passover, and is so called in the calendar, because, according to tradition, the tenth of [*Abib*], when the paschal lamb was to be selected, originally fell on the Sabbath."

This insinuates the story of Israel's miraculous deliverance from the bondage of Egypt began on the Saturday before Passover in like manner as the epic of mankind's deliverance from the bondage of sin began on the Saturday before Passover; when Jesus triumphantly entered into Jerusalem as the Lamb of God who takes away the sins of the world!

---

[289] Exodus 20:10-11, emphasis added
[290] Rabbi Solomon Ganzfried, *The code of Jewish Law – Revised Edition, Vo. 5* (Hebrew Publishing Co., New York, 1961) p.23

Day of Messiah's Public Appearance Foretold

The day of Jesus' Triumphal Entry -- the day when Messiah the King presented Himself to the whole of Israel in the role of the Passover Lamb -- should not have come as a surprise, least of all to the Scribes and Pharisees. While literally hundreds of prophesies within the Hebrew Bible point to Jesus of Nazareth being the Messiah, there's one in particular that's central to dating His public appearance. Over five hundred years prior to the Triumphal Entry, an angel of God delivered a prophecy revealing the exact date it would happen.

In the year 605 BCE, Nebuchadnezzar, king of Babylon, conquered Egypt and continued onward into the kingdom of Judah.[291] The prophet Daniel, a teenager at the time, was taken captive and exiled to Babylon. Sixty-some years later, through studying the *Scroll of Jeremiah*,[292] Daniel came to understand, as a consequence of not keeping the Sabbath, their bondage was to endure a total of seventy years. Being those seventy years were nearly complete, Daniel began to pray and fast on behalf of his countrymen. While confessing

---

[291] 2 Kings 24:7-11; see also "Nebuchadnezzar" *Jewish Encyclopedia*
http://www.JewishEncyclpedia.com/view.jsp?artid=154&letter=N
[292] Jeremiah 25:11–12; 29:10-19

both personal and national sins, the angel Gabriel appeared to Daniel and spoke the following:

> *Know therefore and understand, that from the going forth of the commandment to restore and to build Jerusalem unto the Messiah the Prince shall be seven weeks, and threescore and two weeks: the street shall be built again, and the wall, even in troublous times.*
> *(Daniel 9:25, emphasis added)*

What the angel Gabriel provided Daniel was a mathematical prophecy culminating with the day of Messiah's Triumphal Entry. The word *"weeks"* is derived from the Hebrew word שבוע or *shabuwa* (Strong's #H7620), which means 'period of sevens.' Here it infers 'weeks of years' in reference to a *"Sabbath for the land"* wherein the land is to lie barren every seventh year.[293] Judah's failure to heed this command for 490 years is what instigated their 70 years of captivity in the first place.

A day of prophetic fulfillment is a year in actual time.[294] Therefore, *"Seven [weeks-of-years] and three-score and two [weeks-of-years]"* totals 69 weeks-of-years (7 + 60 + 2); and 69 weeks-of-years totals 483 calendar years (69 X 7).

Furthermore, God established a 360-day calendar year; which most civilizations utilized until about 700 BCE whereupon there

---

[293] 2 Chronicles 36:21; Leviticus 25:1-2; 26:34-35; Deuteronomy 15; Numbers 14:34.
[294] Numbers 14:34 and Ezekiel 4:6.

seems to have been a global change.[295] Nevertheless, civilizations changing calendars doesn't mean God changed calendars. God changes not,[296] and the *Scroll of Revelation* is proof that God will continue to utilize His 360-day calendar year through Messiah's Second Coming.[297]

This is an essential concept to grasp when dealing with prophecy and in this case allows for the calculation of 173,880 days (483 x 360) as being the interval between the commandment to restore and to rebuild Jerusalem, and the presentation (Triumphal Entry) of Messiah the King.[298]

In 586 BCE, after almost twenty years of Babylonian captivity, the kingdom of Judah rebelled again and consequently Nebuchadnezzar's army returned to reduce Jerusalem, and the Temple within, to rubble.[299] Jerusalem remained desolate throughout Daniel's lifetime with no indication of ever being rebuilt. However, over the next one hundred and forty years, four commands/decrees pertaining to its reconstruction were issued.[300] The first three referred primarily to the Temple, but the fourth specifically emphasized the rebuilding of *"the wall."*

---

[295] Assyrians, Carthaginians, Chaldeans, Chinese, Egyptians, Etruscans, Greeks, Hebrews, Hindus, Mayans, Persians, Phoenicians, Teutons; all had 360-day years.
[296] Malachi 3:6; Hebrews 13:8
[297] Revelation 11:2; 12:6; 13:3-4; etc.
[298] First identified in *The Coming Prince* by Sir Robert Anderson (Hodder & Stoughton, London, 1984)
[299] "Temple" *Jewish Encyclopedia*.
http://www.JewishEncyclopedia.com/view.jsp?artid=154&letter=T
[300] Ezra 1:1-4; 6:8-12; 7:12-26; Nehemiah 2:1-8.

By the middle of the 5th century BCE, many of the Hebrew descendants had returned to the land, the Persian monarchy superseded the Babylonian empire, and Nehemiah -- like Joseph and Daniel before him -- was serving in the royal court. Nehemiah was cup-bearer to King Artaxerxes I, a.k.a. Longimanus ("the long handed" reportedly due to a longer right hand).[301] After receiving word of the dire situation in Jerusalem, Nehemiah was willing to forego his prestigious position in order to aid his countrymen.[302] He petitioned King Artaxerxes for the authority to personally oversee the rebuilding of Jerusalem and its wall:

> [1]*And it came to pass in the month of [the Abib], in the twentieth year of Artaxerxes the king, that wine was before him: and I took up the wine, and gave it unto the king. Now I had not been beforetime sad in his presence.* [2]*Wherefore the king said unto me, "Why is thy countenance sad, seeing thou art not sick? This is nothing else but sorrow of heart."*

> *Then I was very sore afraid,* [3]*and said unto the king, "Let the king live forever: why should not my countenance be sad, when the city, the place of my fathers' sepulchers, lieth waste, and the gates thereof are consumed with fire?"* [4]*Then the king said unto me, "For what dost thou make request?"*

---

[301] Nehemiah 1:11-2:1
[302] Nehemiah 1:1-3

So I prayed to the God of heaven. ⁵And I said unto the king, "If it please the king, and if thy servant have found favour in thy sight, that thou wouldest send me unto Judah, unto the city of my fathers' sepulchers, that I may [re]build it." ⁶And the king said unto me (the queen also sitting by him), "For how long shall thy journey be? And when wilt thou return?" So it pleased the king to send me; and I set him a time.

⁷Moreover I said unto the king, "If it please the king, let letters be given me to the governors beyond the river, that they may convey me over till I come into Judah; ⁸And a letter unto Asaph the keeper of the king's forest, that he may give me timber to make beams for the gates of the palace which appertained to the house, <u>and for the wall of the city,</u> and for the house that I shall enter into."

And the king granted me, according to the good hand of my God upon me.
(Nehemiah 2:1-8 emphasis added)

Nehemiah, through his writings,[303] reveals that permission was granted, i.e. command given, to rebuild Jerusalem and its wall by King Artaxerxes during his twentieth year of reign; specifically during the month of the *Abib*.

---

[303] Evidence suggests Ezra was the Nehemiah's scribe. Ezra and Nehemiah are traditionally compiled within a single book.

Confusion can arise from Nehemiah 1:1-2 wherein translations cast the implemented calendar system into doubt. It can appear as if the month of *Chislev* (Nov/Dec) occurs before the month of the *Abib* (Mar/Apr), and thereby incorrectly implies the use of the Civil Calendar (autumn-to-autumn). Yet Nehemiah 8:14-17 records the Feast of Tabernacles being in the seventh month, which inarguably validates the Religious Calendar (spring-to-spring) as the system in use. Likewise, the *Scroll of Ezra* and *Scroll of Esther,* written in the same era, both utilize the Religious Calendar.[304]

The confusion, yet again, is the result of translation. The King James Version, as do most, mistakenly renders the opening verses of Nehemiah in the following manner:

> *The words of Nehemiah, the son of Hachaliah. And it came to pass in the month Chislev, in the twentieth year, as I was in Shushan the palace, that Hanani, one of my brethren, came, he and certain men of Judah... (Nehemiah 1:1-2)*

Lost in translation is Nehemiah's opening statement which essentially proclaims, 'The record of events in the twentieth year of Artaxerxes;' and thereafter reverts

---

[304] Dating Nehemiah is further achieved via the Elephantine papyri and Samaritan papyri; documents from the 5th century BCE written in Imperial Aramaic bearing strong stylistic resemblance to Aramaic documents in Ezra.

back to the month of *Chislev* of the previous year in laying foundation for the noteworthy events in the twentieth year which start with chapter two. This is exemplified in the *International Standard Version:*[305]

> *In this document, I, Hacaliah's son Nehemiah, recount what occurred in the twentieth year of Artaxerxes:*
>
> *During the month of Chislev, while I was in Shushan at the palace, Hanani, one of my brothers, arrived with some men from Judah... (Nehemiah 1:1-2, ISV)*

Chapter two opens: *"And it came to pass in the month of [the Abib], in the twentieth year of Artaxerxes the king."* This substantiates the events of chapter one as preceding Artaxerxes' twentieth year, otherwise this declaration would be needlessly redundant.[306]

So with the Religious Calendar (spring-to-spring) established as the calendar system implemented within the *Scroll of Nehemiah*, the next step in dating Artaxerxes' decree to restore and rebuild Jerusalem is to determine the twentieth year of Artaxerxes' reign.

---

[305] Upon personal correspondence with *ISV* translators, the rendering was implemented.

[306] Nehemiah's subsequent references to months (8:2, 9:1) don't reassert it as being the twentieth year of Artaxerxes

History records that King Artaxerxes ascended to the throne on the equivalent of December 19, 465 BCE; upon the death of his father, King Ahasuerus (married to Queen Esther).[307] In actuality, King Ahasuerus was murdered by the commander of his bodyguard, by a man named *Artabanus*.[308] *Artabanus* succeeded King Ahasuerus to the throne and reigned for seven months before being killed by Artaxerxes; the third son of King Ahasuerus. As the legitimate heir to the throne, Artaxerxes retroactively commenced his reign from the date of his father's death in order to remove any memory of the usurper.

Therefore, King Artaxerxes' first year of reign is reckoned from his father's death in December of 465 BCE until the Persian New Year in the spring of 464 BCE, whereupon Artaxerxes' second year of reign commenced.

Calculating forward, King Artaxerxes' twentieth year of reign began in the spring of 446 BCE. Thus, it was during the month of the *Abib* in the spring of 446 BCE when King Artaxerxes issued the foreordained command to restore and rebuild Jerusalem, and the clock started counting down the 173,880 days until Messiah's scheduled Triumphal Entry.

After factoring in all of the necessary conversions, the 7th day in the month of the *Abib* (March 28th), 446 BCE, to the 10th day in the month of the *Abib* (April 21st), 31 CE, fulfills Daniel's 69-weeks to the very day!

---

[307] *King Ahasuerus* is also known by the Greek rendering of *King Xerxes*. He ruled over the Persian Empire from 486-465 BCE.

[308] http://www.britannica.com/EBchecked/topic/36682/Artabanus

Calculations: from 446 BCE to 31 CE is 476 years (no year zero); multiplying 476 years by 365 days (solar calendar year) equates to 173,740; adding 116 days to account for leap years (one day for every fourth year except century years not divisible by 400) totals 173,856; and, finally, adding calendar 24 days (March 28th to April 21st) sums up to 173,880.

Daniel's 69-Weeks Prophecy

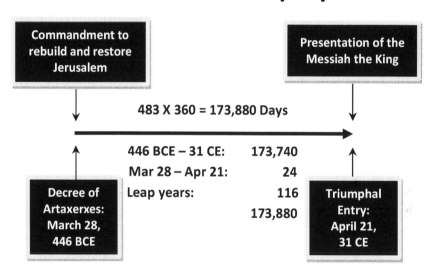

Jesus' "Public Appearance" as Messiah riding an untamed colt of a donkey into Jerusalem, as foretold by the prophet Zechariah, occurred 173,880 days after the command to restore and rebuild Jerusalem, as foretold by the prophet Daniel -- on Saturday, April 21, 31 CE.

This was first identified by Sir Robert Anderson (*The Coming Prince*, 1894) wherein he dates Artaxerxes' 20th year of reign to coincide with the 20th year since his father's death in 445 BCE instead of after 19 years in 446 BCE.

While some may be skeptical that Daniel's 69-weeks can be broken down into the exact number of days, precedent was set during Israel's exodus from Egypt:

> And it came to pass at the end of the four hundred and thirty years, <u>even the selfsame day it came to pass</u>, that all the hosts of the LORD went out from the land of Egypt.
> (Exodus 12:40-41, emphasis added)

This constitutes an astonishing fulfillment of prophecy which is neither the result of chance nor coincidence, but is the unmistakable product of intelligent design; wholly conceived and executed by an omnipotent God who orchestrates world events from outside the dimension of time. It's through the fulfillment of such prophecy that God authenticates His Word down through the ages. God inhabits eternity.[309] He knows the beginning from the end, and He relays this fact through His prophets with stunning accuracy.

The Passover of 31 CE was historically advocated as the year Messiah's crucifixion by several of the early Church Fathers including Eusebius of Caesarea (c. 263 – 339),[310] Aurelius Cassiodorus (c. 485 – 585),[311] and Maximus the Confessor (c. 580 – 662).[312]

---

[309] Isaiah 57:15

[310] http://en.wikipedia.org/wiki/Eusebius_of_Caesarea

[311] Hales, William (1830), *A New Analysis of Chronology and Geography, History and Prophecy*. 1. p. 70.

[312] http://en.wikipedia.org/wiki/Maximus_the_Confessor

Literal Rendering of Daniel 9:26

In contemplating another layer of Daniel's 70-Week prophecy, a provocative hypothesis emerges with a literal rendering of Daniel 9:26 -- *"And after threescore and two weeks shall Messiah be cut off."* If Messiah's ministry entailed 62 literal weeks leading up to His crucifixion amid the fourth week of April in 31 CE, then the start of His ministry would've been the third week of February in 30 CE. This fits comfortably within the parameters and chronological record of a 13- to 19 month (yearling) ministry.

Even more provocative, if Messiah was baptized 62 weeks prior to Passion Week -- Sunday, February 12th, 30 CE -- and He entered into the wilderness to endure 40 days of temptation that evening at sunset -- Monday, February 13th, 30 CE -- then the 40th and final day came to pass on Friday, March 24th, 30 CE. This is significant because that evening is most likely when the new moon was sighted (illumination about 3%), and the New Year in the month of the *Abib* was declared.

The big picture: when Jesus completed Satan's final temptation upon the pinnacle of the Temple[313] at the end of the 40th day (sunset), cheers of rejoicing immediately rang out as the moon was sighted and the New Year -- *"the acceptable year of the* LORD*"*[314] -- was heralded throughout the Promised Land!

---

[313] Luke 4:9-12
[314] Luke 4:16-21

Prophetic Accountability

Returning to the events which encompass the Triumphal Entry on Saturday the 10th day in the month of the *Abib*, as Jesus rode upon the colt of a donkey down from the Mount of Olives towards Jerusalem, He looked out over the city, began to weep, and made a startling prophetic announcement:

> Saying, 'If thou [Jerusalem] hadst known, even thou, at least <u>in this thy day</u>, the things which belong unto thy peace! But now they are hid from thine eyes. For the days shall come upon thee, that thine enemies shall cast a trench about thee, and compass thee round, and keep thee in on every side, and shall lay thee even with the ground, and thy children within thee; and they shall not leave in thee one stone upon another; because <u>thou knewest not the time of thy visitation</u>.' (Luke 19:42-44, emphasis added)

Jesus herein holds the children of Israel accountable to know Daniel's 69-Weeks prophecy; He holds them accountable to know on that specific date the Messiah is scheduled to appear; He expects them to know on Saturday, the 10th day in the month of the *Abib* of that year, He would triumphantly enter as the rightful heir to the Throne of David! As a consequence of their ignorance, Jesus foretold Jerusalem would again be destroyed and the Temple dismantled stone by stone.

True to His word, in 69 CE, Jerusalem was invaded by the fifth, tenth, twelfth, and fifteenth Roman legions under Titus Vespasian.[315] A year later, Jerusalem was utterly defeated; over one million inhabitants lay dead in the streets. Josephus, the first-century Jewish-Roman historian, describes the devastation: "It was so thoroughly laid even with the ground by those that dug it up to the foundation that there was left nothing to make those that came thither believe it had ever been inhabited."[316]

On the 9th of *Av* (August 4th or 5th), 70 CE, the defenders were over-run and the Temple set ablaze.[317] The Temple interior, which constituted little more than acacia wood overlaid with gold, was totally consumed in the fire. Subsequently, in order to recover the gold which melted and seeped into the cracks, the Temple was literally dismantled stone by stone!

Josephus comments: "They carried away every stone of the sacred Temple, partially in a frenzied search for every last piece of gold ornamentation melted in the awful heat of the fire. They also plowed the ground level, and since it had already been sown with its defenders' blood, they sowed it with salt."[318]

---

[315] "Titus Vespasianus." BBC. 2004.
http://www.bbc.co.uk.historic_figures/titus.shtml
[316] Josephus, *The Wars of the Jews* (VII.1,1)
[317] Believed to be the same date Nebuchadnezzar destroyed the Solomon's Temple.
[318] Josephus, *The Wars of the Jews*.

Although the second Temple was inferior to the magnificence of Solomon's Temple, the prophet Haggai foretold *"The glory of this latter house shall be greater than of the former."*[319] This was understood to mean that Messiah would enter into the second Temple. Therefore, upon its destruction, Jerusalem was full of sorrow and wailing; in part because the city lay desolate and loved ones lay dead, but in part because the Temple had been destroyed and the Messiah, so they thought, had not come.

Yet the inhabitants of Jerusalem were wrong; the Messiah had come. Thirty-nine and one-half years earlier, the Messiah openly presented Himself riding upon the colt of a donkey as He triumphantly entered through the East Gate on Saturday the 10th day in the month of the *Abib*; four days prior to His burial at evening on Wednesday the 14th day in the month of the *Abib*, and one week prior to His resurrection at evening on Saturday the 17th day in the month of the *Abib*.

Daniel's Prophecy Historically Recognized

Although the full scope of Daniel's prophecy is 70 weeks, 69 weeks encompasses the interval between the decree to rebuild Jerusalem and Messiah's public appearance. Thereafter, there's an indeterminate gap between the 69th and 70th week (after which Messiah makes His second public appearance). Nevertheless, while some scholars deny Daniel's

---

[319] Haggai 2:2-9

mathematical properties, there's historical evidence of its long accepted application:

- ❖ *Babylonian Talmud* -- a repository of written and oral laws with extensive commentary, completed in the 7th century CE, which includes various notations about Messiah's coming. Rabbi *Judah haNasi*, a key compiler, wrote in regards to Daniel's prophecy and the Messiah's expected appearance, "These times were over long ago."[320]

  In despair, rabbis sanctioned a curse upon all whom calculated the time of Messiah's coming: "May they drop [dead] who try to figure out the end; for they say, since the time of his coming has already arrived yet he did not come, therefore he will not come at all."[321]

- ❖ Rabbi Moses Ben Maimon (Maimonides) -- Jewish sage who lived in the twelfth-century and is one of the most respected rabbis of all time. He conceded, "Daniel has elucidated to us the knowledge of the end times. However, since they are secret, the wise have barred the calculation of the days of Messiah's coming so that the untutored populace will not be led astray when they see that the End Times have already come but there is no sign of the Messiah."[322]

---

[320] Talmud, *Sanhedrin*, 98b and 97a.
[321] Ibid, *Sanhedrin* 97b
[322] *Igeret Teiman*, Chapter 3 p.24.

❖ The Qumran community -- from where the *Dead Sea Scrolls* originate. Documentation proves they, too, believed Daniel's 69-Weeks prophecy equates to a mathematical calculation of Messiah's appearance.[323]

It's astounding how scholarly people so intimate with Scripture can fail to recognize the historical fulfillment of Messianic prophecies within the person of Jesus of Nazareth. Prophecy is not generic in the sense that it can be selectively interpreted. In the case of the Messiah's coming, there are strict time constraints in regards to when He must appear. It's ironic how people who believe with all their heart, mind, and soul that Scripture is infallible, at the same time accept the difficult position that, contrary to Scripture, Messiah has yet to come.

Yet the sword cuts both ways: it's also astounding how people who recognize Jesus to be the Messiah accept the preposterous position that, contrary to Scripture, He failed to fulfill His sign of three days and three nights in the heart of the earth!

---

[323] *Biblical Archaeological Review*, Nov/Dec 1992, p.58.

Chapter Eight
Holidays vs. Appointed Times

Stand in the ways and see, and ask for the old paths where the good way is, and walk in it; Then you will find rest for your souls. But they said, 'We will not walk in it.' (Jeremiah 6:16)

Mixing of Spiritual Seed

The celebratory history of Good Friday – Easter Sunday can be traced back as far as 1900 years, though noteworthy is the fact nowhere in Scripture is there precedent to observe these days. In truth, such teachings were devised by men who had no authority to do so. The practice of mixing *"traditions of men"* with the worship of the one true God is an ongoing theme of contention throughout Scripture; and given some of the repercussions God has inflicted upon those celebrating man-made holidays, traditions like Good Friday – Easter Sunday can prove exceedingly dangerous.

The more stark examples include the children of Israel while upon Mount Sinai creating a new holiday to God whereupon the whole assembly was nearly incinerated, although Moses intervened and only 3,000 were slain.[324] Also, Israel's King Jeroboam implemented a new holiday to God *"devised of his own heart"[325]* whereupon his entire family was annihilated[326]

---

[324] Exodus 32
[325] 1 Kings 12:33

and the Northern Kingdom was sent into exile.[327] The God of Abraham, Isaac, and Jacob is extremely protective of His statutes and precepts, and mankind is not to add nor subtract from them.[328] The Almighty seeks pure unadulterated worship, and yet humanity continually feels the need to incorporate his own religious methodology.

Amid His short ministry, Jesus personally decried mankind's insistence on worshipping God Almighty in his own way:

> 'Howbeit in vain do they worship Me, teaching [for] doctrines the commandments of men. For laying aside the commandment of God, ye hold the tradition of men, [as] the washing of pots and cups: and many other such like things ye do.' And He said unto them, 'Full well ye reject the commandment of God, that ye may keep your own tradition.' (Mark 7:7-9)

If that doesn't convey the seriousness of this issue, nothing will. *"Traditions of men"* have no place in the worship of God; neither contrived ceremonies, sacraments, nor esoteric rites. God abhors the integration of man-made rituals and customs with His revealed Word. God desires to be worshipped in spirit and truth,[329] and with all one's heart, strength, mind, and soul.

---

[326] 1 Kings 13:34; 14:10-11
[327] 1 Kings 14:15-16
[328] Deuteronomy 12:32
[329] John 4:23-24

Infiltration of the Church

The strategy of Lucifer, that dragon of old, has always been to corrupt and to destroy. Satan has tried to contaminate the royal bloodline so as to destroy the lineage of Messiah, and he has tried to pervert the truth so as to corrupt man's knowledge and worship of the Almighty. Satan has repeatedly tried to exterminate the Jews as well as to stamp out the Church. While he's failed in these ventures, he's nonetheless succeeded in perpetuating a people who call themselves Jews but are not, and in infiltrating the churches so as to accost Messiah's character through the mingling of false doctrines, *Talmudic* regulations, and "Christianized" pagan customs.

In relating how all *untruth*, no matter how seemingly insignificant, detrimentally impacts the perfect character of Messiah, the late Dr. Walter Martin imparts an excellent summary in his classic reference-work, *Kingdom of the Cults:* "Since the earliest days of Christianity, both apostle and disciple alike have been confronted with the perversion of the revelation God has given us in the person of Jesus. This perversion has extended historically, not just to the teachings of our LORD, but more important, in the Person of Christ; for it is axiomatic that if the doctrine of Christ Himself, i.e. His Person, nature, and work are perverted, so the identity of the Life-giver is altered, then the life which He came to give is correspondingly negated... And if Jesus' [character and works are] redefined and interpreted out of context and therefore contrary to its Biblical content, the whole message of the

Gospel is radically altered and its value correspondingly diminished."[330]

In guarding against attacks upon Messiah's perfect character, doctrine is to perpetually be reaffirmed: *"Prove all things; hold fast [only] that which is good;"*[331] truth is to be continually reproved: *"Prove what is that good and acceptable and perfect will of God;"*[332] and false doctrine is to be publicly exposed as heresy so as to prevent the masses from being surreptitiously persuaded: *"...have no fellowship with the unfruitful works of darkness, but rather reprove [them]."*[333]

These proved themselves to be important principles as the battle for Scriptural truth soon boiled over. It was no surprise when the young assemblies of the early centuries found themselves under fierce spiritual attack. They were intentionally targeted, just as Biblically-sound assemblies are today. Jesus forewarned:

> *Beware of false prophets, which come to you*
> *in sheep's clothing but inwardly are ravening*
> *wolves. (Matthew 7:15)*

Even within the apostles' own lifetimes, many false prophets and false doctrines crept into circulation. In attempting to get their Messianic brethren to open their eyes to such deceptions

---

[330] Dr. Walter Martin – *The Kingdom of the Cults* (Minneapolis, Bethany House Publishers, revised and expanded edition – 1985) pp.377-378
[331] 1 Thessalonians 5:21
[332] Romans 12:2
[333] Ephesians 5:11

and hold fast to the Scriptures, the apostle Paul chastised the assembly in Galatia:

> *I marvel that ye are so soon removed from Him that called you into the grace of Christ unto another Gospel: which is not another; but there be some that trouble you, and would pervert the Gospel of Christ.*
> *(Galatians 1:6-7)*

In the meantime, the offensive against the assemblies intensified while agents-of-change corrupted the Gospel by working their way up through church hierarchy into positions of influence. The apostles tirelessly combated the assault of false doctrines, and repeatedly issued warnings among the assemblies to remain alert towards those smooth talking deceivers who pervert the Word of God:

> *Now I urge you, brethren, to watch out for those who create divisions and sinful enticements in opposition to the teachings you have learned [from us]. Stay away from them! For such people are not serving Christ our Lord but their own desires.*
> *(Romans 16:17)*

> *Beware lest any man spoil you through philosophy and vain deceit, after the tradition of men, after the rudiments of the world, and not after Christ. (Colossians 2:8)*

197

Yet because prior generations failed to heed the instructions of Scripture and warnings of the apostles -- as did the assembly in Berea[334] -- churches now find themselves in the doctrinal mire that they do. But this, too, was foreseeable and foretold. The apostles knew an onslaught of false teachings would work their way into the mainstream and erode at doctrinal truths:

> *For the time will come when people [Christians] will not endure sound doctrine; but after their own lusts shall they heap to themselves teachers, having itching ears; and they shall turn away their ears from the truth, and shall be turned unto fables.*
> *(2 Timothy 4:3-4)*

The preceding passage isn't directed toward any particular false teaching, but rather the general trend of Christianity as a whole to fall away from God's commandments towards doctrines which are audibly pleasing but with no basis in fact. The apostasy was inevitable, and yet the apostles went to their deaths sounding the alarm as watchmen on the wall:

> *Also of your own selves shall men arise, speaking perverse things, to draw away disciples after them. Therefore watch, and remember, that by the space of three years I ceased not to warn every one night and day with tears. (Acts 20:30-31)*

---

[334] Acts 17:11

Tradition that Denies the LORD

The apostle Peter foretold that false teachings would be introduced into the assemblies, and overwhelmingly accepted; however, he added that the masses would eventually come to accept certain false teachings so bold as to inherently deny Jesus as Lord.

> But there were false prophets also among the people [in Old Testament times], even as there shall be false teachers among you, who privily shall bring in damnable heresies, _even denying the Lord who bought them,_ and bring upon themselves swift destruction. And many shall follow their pernicious ways; by reason of whom the Way of truth shall be evil spoken of.
> (2 Peter 2:1-2, emphasis added)

Of all the false teachings that fit into this abominable category (the non-deity of Messiah, the Mary Magdalene Heresy, etc.), without question the one that has gained the greatest acceptance, the one that has deceived literally hundreds of millions of people, is the Good Friday – Easter Sunday tradition. It's a false teaching that blasphemes the true duration Jesus remained entombed; and it's a false teaching that, to this day, perpetuates the lie Jesus failed to fulfill the sign He offered as miraculous proof that He's the Messiah; the Anointed One of the Most High.

In analyzing Peter's admonition, there are three criteria by which to identify, and subsequently re-verify, this most detestable of false teachings:

> ➤ <u>One</u> – it's a teaching that, as of the first-century, was yet to be introduced into the assemblies (the Good Friday – Easter Sunday tradition didn't become official doctrine until the fourth-century).

> ➤ <u>Two</u> – it's a teaching that denies the Lord (the Good Friday – Easter Sunday tradition denies who Jesus is by denying He fulfilled the *Sign of Jonah*).

> ➤ <u>Three</u> – it's a teaching that, for whatever reason, becomes accepted by the *"many"* (the Good Friday – Easter Sunday tradition is tremendously popular, so much so that even non-Christians partake in its festivities).

Admittedly, no amount of good works will ever merit the reward of eternal life; it's exclusively the gift of the Almighty through the redeeming blood of Jesus, the Passover Lamb of God. Nevertheless, those who honor Good Friday – Easter Sunday while professing Jesus is Savior with their lips are unknowingly denying Jesus is Savior through their works when observing this devised commandment of men.

> *This people draweth nigh unto Me with their mouth, and honoureth Me with [their] lips; but their heart is far from Me. But in vain they do worship Me, teaching [for] doctrines the commandments of men.*
> *(Matthew 15:8-9)*

Don't be offended this is being called out for correction; be offended by having been taught this sacrilege in the first place. It's a travesty that denominations continue to take the populace position of filling pews over their responsibility as shepherds to disseminate the truth.

If the churches refuse to correct it from the top down, then believers need to affect change from the bottom up. Outside of Catholicism, neither Palm Sunday nor Good Friday is a huge ordeal, so expunging them from *Doctrinal Statements* and eliminating them from observance isn't an insurmountable task. Talk it up, challenge the parishioners, and approach the deacons and elders.

Yet don't misunderstand the larger issue: this isn't a call to commemorate Wednesday in lieu of Friday. This isn't about a commemorating a specific day of the week at all. Messiah's Wednesday crucifixion is merely historical fact demonstrating He fulfilled the *sign of Jonah*. The true commemoration of His death is found in the New Covenant Passover, and the true celebration of His sacrifice being accepted by God the Father post-resurrection is found in the New Covenant feast of First-fruits.

Never heard of the New Covenant application of these feasts? It's not surprising given the Church's heavy-handed insistence that everyone recognize its self-serving version of Passion Week. But these are Biblical feasts which Jesus and the apostles kept throughout their entire lifetimes, and so did most of the early church for 300 years after His ascension. Moreover, they're feast days with Scriptural precedent per mandate of Deuteronomy-13, so they aren't additions to the Scriptural record. To the contrary, they're occasions that originally foreshadowed, and now commemorate, the very events which Christendom holds so dear.

The Feasts of the LORD

When God descended upon Mount Sinai in fire, He revealed the rules and precepts by which His people are to live. This entailed instructions on how to love and respect one another as well as instructions on how to love and worship Him. In addition to the Ten Commandments, God revealed His principles of good health, His system of justice, and His days of holy convocations. Although they're often slanderously misrepresented as "feasts of Moses" and "feasts of the Jews," Scripture refers to these as *"feasts of the LORD."* As can be seen, God clearly asserts ownership of them:

> *... say unto them [concerning] the feasts of the LORD which ye shall proclaim [to be] holy convocations, 'These are My feasts' ... These*

are the feasts of the LORD holy convocations which ye shall proclaim in their seasons. (Leviticus 23:2 & 4)

Through His servant Moses, God relays His feasts which He commands be kept as perpetual ordinances from generation to generation;[335] some in the spring corresponding to Messiah's First Coming, and some in the autumn corresponding to Messiah's Second Coming.

Fulfilling the abundant shadow-pictures in the Hebrew Bible (Old Testament) as well as the prophetic implications within the *feasts of the* LORD is the context of Jesus' proclamation:

Think not that I am come to destroy the Law or the prophets; I am not come to destroy, but to fulfill. (Matthew 5:17)

The Hebrew word for *"feasts"* is מוֹעֵד or *mow`ed* (Strong's #H4150), and actually means *"Appointed Times."* God's feasts/Appointed Times are dates designated as momentous occasions within His master plan for human sanctification. They're essentially divine appointments which God scheduled beforehand so that His people would habitually assemble on these days and therein be ready for their grander fulfillment when they come to pass.

---

[335] Exodus 12:14-24, 31:13-16; Leviticus 16:29-31

New Covenant Appointed Times

- **Passover** -- Messiah's death as the Lamb of God
- **Feast of Unleavened Bread** -- obedience to God's commands; eliminating sin from one's life
- **First-fruits** -- God's acceptance of Messiah as the First-fruits of all who shall be born into eternity
- **Pentecost** -- the pouring out of the Holy Spirit
- **Feast of Trumpets** -- Messiah's Second Coming
- **Day of Atonement** -- God and His people being at one; Satan bound for 1000 years
- **Feast of Tabernacles** -- Messiah's millennial reign
- **Last Great Day** -- the Great White Throne Judgment

At what point in history did God schedule these *mow`ed,* i.e. these divine Appointed Times? The answer is found within the creation account of Genesis chapter one:

> *And God said, "Let there be lights in the firmament of the heaven to divide the day from the night; and let them be for signs, and for seasons [mow`ed], and for days, and years." (Genesis 1:14)*

These feasts were designated as Appointed Times from before the foundations of the world! In actuality, Genesis 1:14 ought to be translated, "...*Let them be for signs, and for appointed times, and for days, and years.*"

In Hebrew, the words *"holy convocations"* are מִקְרָא קֹדֶשׁ or *miqra' qodesh* (Strong's #H4744 and #H6944), meaning something called out; i.e. a public meeting (the act, the persons, or the place); <u>also a rehearsal</u> -- assemblies, callings, or meetings by appointment.

In other words, God's Sabbaths are a public calling out; *appointed times* for God's people to assemble and rehearse for the ultimate fulfillment of these holy convocations which mark essential steps in the process of human sanctification. Furthermore, keeping and honoring these Sabbaths constitutes a sign between God and His people:

> *Moreover also I gave them My Sabbaths, to be a sign between Me and them, that they might know that I am the Lord that sanctify them... (Ezekiel 20:12).*

In contrast to God's Appointed Times which are rehearsals, memorials, and a sign, consider what the Almighty has to say about man's calendar system and man's devised holidays such as Good Friday – Easter Sunday as well as others:

> *Your New Moons [calendar] and your appointed feasts [holidays] My soul hateth; they are a trouble unto Me. (Isaiah 1:14)*

Observing God's Appointed Times is serious business, and the responsibility of justification and verification falls upon each individual who partakes. While truly understanding the gravity and depth of the *Feasts of the LORD* is a comprehensive study in itself, the following is an overview of the spring feasts entailing the celebration and commemoration of Messiah's crucifixion and resurrection:

Passover

Although it's a wonderful testimony to the God of Israel, the Hebrews' deliverance from the bondage of slavery in Egypt isn't the ultimate significance of the Passover. Recall that it was after they departed Egypt and were upon Mount Sinai when God instructed the Hebrews to annually observe Passover as both a memorial and a rehearsal. The Passover of Moses was yet another shadow-picture of grander fulfillment that would come to pass on that very date some 1500 years later when God's people were delivered from the bondage of sin through the redeeming blood of the Lamb of God.

Just as households in Egypt whose doorposts were marked by the blood of a lamb were the only ones *"passed over"* by the Angel of Death, so those at the Great White Throne Judgment whose sins are covered by the blood of the Lamb will be the only ones exempt from the second death.

In reference to animal sacrifices (lambs, goats, bulls, oxen, doves, etc.), their blood never truly atoned for sin. The Levitical system of sacrifice was likewise a shadow-picture and a schoolmaster pointing to the Messiah who would assume the role of the Passover Lamb sacrificed on behalf of mankind:

> But in those [animal sacrifices is] a remembrance again of sins every year. _For [it's] not possible that the blood of bulls and of goats should take away [human] sins._ (Hebrews 10:3-4, emphasis added)

> And every priest standeth daily ministering and offering oftentimes the same sacrifices, _which can never take away sins_: But this Man, after He had offered one sacrifice for sins for ever, sat down on the right hand of God. (Hebrews 10:9-12, emphasis added)

Animal blood is not a substitute for human blood. Only the righteous blood of a sinless man can atone for the sins of another man. However, no-one is without sin -- _"for all have sinned, and come short of the glory of God"_[336] -- and so one man's blood is incapable of atoning for another man's sin:

> No man can by any means redeem his brother or give to God a ransom for him - for the redemption of his soul is costly... (Psalm 49:7-8)

---

[336] Romans 3:23

Even if it were possible, the righteous blood of a sinless man could only atone for one other man (of equal value). Therefore, only the righteous blood of a sinless Man of greater value than the whole of mankind (their Creator) can atone for the sins of all mankind:

> For what the Law could not do, in that it was weak through the flesh, God sending His own Son in the likeness of sinful flesh, and for sin, condemned sin in the flesh. (Romans 8:3)

The righteous blood of God-in-the-flesh shed on behalf of mankind as payment for the sins of the world is the ultimate fulfillment of Passover to which the shadow-pictures of the exodus from Egypt, animal sacrifices, the High Priest and Levitical priesthood, the selection of a lamb without spot or blemish, Abraham's sacrifice of Isaac, and others all point:

> But Christ being come a High Priest of good things to come, by a greater and more perfect tabernacle not made with hands, that is to say, not of this building; neither by the blood of goats and calves, but by His own blood He entered in once into the Holy Place, having obtained eternal redemption [for us]. (Hebrews 9:11-12)

The preceding verses reveal that the Temple in Jerusalem was likewise a model and shadow-picture of the true heavenly Tabernacle to be revealed when the New Jerusalem is brought down from heaven at the end of the Sabbath millennium.[337] Additionally, in setting up the earthly Tabernacle, Moses prepared its furnishings "...*according to the [heavenly] pattern for them which [he was] being shown on the mountain.*"[338]

It seems everything in the scrolls of Moses are an elaborate worldly replica of the yet greater heavenly realm which awaits those who love the God and keep His commandments.[339]

Comprehension of these shadow-pictures adds perspective to a statement made by the apostle Paul, who is too often quoted out of context:

> *Wherefore the Law was our schoolmaster [to bring us] unto Christ, that we might be justified by faith. But after that faith is come, we are no longer under a schoolmaster. (Galatians 3:24-25)*

Paul isn't advocating that the Law (of God by the hand of Moses) was rendered obsolete through Messiah, but that the Law essentially served as a schoolmaster in preparing God's people to comprehend the fuller meaning of the Almighty's instructions and feasts which would be revealed in Messiah.

It wasn't irony that Jesus was crucified on Passover, nor was it fortuitous coincidence. To the contrary, it was the ultimate

---

[337] Revelation 21:2
[338] Exodus 25:40
[339] I John 5:3; Revelation 14:12

fulfillment of this holy convocation for which God's people had been rehearsing since the time of Moses!

> ... *For even Christ, our Passover, is sacrificed*
> *for us. Therefore, let us keep the feast...*
> *(1 Corinthians 5:7-8)*

Paul was writing to Gentile believers in Corinth about keeping the Messianic context of the feasts of the LORD some 20 years after the crucifixion![340] With the Egyptian Passover paling in comparison to Messiah's achievement as *"the [Passover] Lamb of God which taketh away the sin of the world,"*[341] the apostles and assemblies continued to observe Passover on the 14th day in the month of the *Abib*; although no longer as a rehearsal for a grander event, but in commemoration of Messiah's sacrificial death which allowed them exodus from the bondage of spiritual Egypt.

Today, with 2000 years having elapsed between the crucifixion and the twenty-first century, Messiah's ultimate sacrifice as the Lamb of God, *"our Passover,"* is no less an occasion to commemorate. Instead of superficially paying homage to a fabled 'Good Friday,' prayerfully

---

[340] Paul's first epistle to the Corinthians is believed to have been written between 53- and 57 CE.
[341] John 1:29

consider observing the New Covenant Passover in the same manner as did the apostles and early church.

Commemorating Passover doesn't mean sacrificing a lamb and rubbing its blood upon the doorposts; for that, too, is a shadow-picture long since fulfilled. Foremost, commemorating Passover means acknowledging the true date of Messiah's crucifixion, and recognizing the fulfillment of God's *Appointed Time* wherein the first step toward human sanctification was achieved. In recognition of this, Passover is the final day to purge the leavening from one's home in preparation for the Feast of Unleavened Bread which begins at evening following Passover.

Additionally, Passover is the appropriate time to partake in communion; after all, it's the very date upon which Messiah instituted the New Covenant symbols of bread and wine as being representative of His body and His blood:

> *And as they were eating, Jesus took bread and blessed, and brake [it], and gave [it] to the disciples, and said, 'Take, eat; this is My body.' And He took the cup, and gave thanks, and gave [it] to them, saying, 'Drink ye all of it; for this is My blood of the new covenant, which is shed for many for the remission of sins.' (Matthew 26:26-28)*

Another option is to seek out a Messianic Seder. There are congregations throughout the country which open up their doors for this memorable meal which showcases the Seder, too, being a shadow-picture of Messiah's death and resurrection.

Feast of Unleavened Bread

The Feast of Unleavened Bread is a seven day feast immediately following Passover. As mentioned earlier, Passover is the preparation day for high Sabbath which kicks off the Feast of Unleavened Bread on the 15th day in the month of the *Abib,* no matter what day of the week. Passover and the Feast of Unleavened Bread are inseparable. The lamb sacrificed and prepared on the Passover was to be eaten during the first evening of the Feast of Unleavened Bread.

Although not required, the first evening of the Feast of Unleavened Bread is still a suitable occasion to enjoy lamb for supper. This is what the Hebrews of old ate every year on this date for the better part

of 1500 years until the destruction of the Temple in 70 CE. Eating lamb in itself doesn't constitute a Levitical sacrifice; it's simply an acknowledgement of Jesus as the Lamb of God having been sacrificed for sin on the Passover.

The instruction to observe the Feast of Unleavened Bread was relayed by God through Moses upon Mount Sinai. Like Passover, its preliminary meaning relates back to Israel's exodus from Egypt. The Hebrews were commanded to leave in haste without allowing their freshly made dough to rise.

> *And Moses said unto the people, "Remember this day [the fifteenth day in the month of the Abib], in which ye came out from Egypt, out of the house of bondage; for by strength of hand* the LORD *brought you out from this [place]: there shall no leavened bread be eaten. This day came ye out in the month [of the] Abib... Seven days thou shalt eat unleavened bread, and in the seventh day [shall be] a feast to the* LORD. *Unleavened bread shall be eaten seven days; and there shall no leavened bread be seen with thee, neither shall there be leaven seen with thee in all thy quarters. Thou shalt keep this ordinance in its season from year to year."* (Exodus 13:3-10)

Scripturally, leaven is symbolic of sin; and so the grander meaning of the Feast of Unleavened Bread is evident. After accepting Messiah's sacrificial death (Passover) on account of personal sin, one must thereafter rid his/her life of sinful behavior (Feast of Unleavened Bread). The communal effect of both the Passover and the Feast of Unleavened Bread is exemplified in a statement Jesus made to a prostitute whom

He spared from being stoned to death: *"Neither do I condemn thee [Passover]. Go, and sin no more [Feast of Unleavened Bread]."*[342]

Jesus further invoked this metaphor when He warned:

> *"...beware of the leaven of the Pharisees and of the Sadducees." (Matthew 16:6)*

This is the modern equivalent of warning to beware of religious authorities demanding adherence to false doctrines and antiquated rituals which manifest a worldly appearance of Godliness but in fact are contrary to the revealed Word of the living God.

The apostle Paul also utilized this leaven-as-sin metaphor in chastising the Gentile believers in Galatia who had become tolerant of seemingly trivial unscriptural matters:

> *Ye did run well; who did hinder you that ye should not obey the truth? This persuasion [cometh] not of Him that calleth you. A little leaven leaveneth the whole lump.*
> *(Galatians 5:7-9, emphasis added)*

Moreover, in re-addressing Paul's statement to *"keep the feast"* per 1 Corinthians 5, the feast Paul alludes to keeping is the Feast of Unleavened Bread.

---

[342] John 8:11

214

In its leaven-as-sin context, the full excerpt is as follows:

> *...Know ye not that a little leaven leaveneth the whole lump? Purge out therefore the old leaven, that ye may be a new lump, as ye are unleavened. For even Christ, our Passover, is sacrificed for us: Therefore let us keep the feast, not with old leaven, neither with the leaven of malice and wickedness; but with the unleavened [bread] of sincerity and truth. (1 Corinthians 5:6-8)*

Leaven is also symbolic of malice, wickedness, deceit, and all that is contrary to love and truth. Aside from observing the Feast of Unleavened Bread for seven days, the implication is that all believers must attempt to live "unleavened" lives.

Seven is the Scriptural number of completeness; therefore, observing the Feast of Unleavened Bread for seven days is symbolic of the complete doing away of sin. It's a worthy goal even if it proves impossible. Similarly, ridding leaven from one's life for a week proves difficult. To partake in this seven day feast is to endure a week of perpetual temptation; a symbolic reminder of the need to stop transgressing the laws of the Almighty. Eliminating leavened products from one's diet for seven days is a shadow-picture of eliminating sin from one's life. Of course, the ultimate fulfillment of the Feast of Unleavened Bread won't come until His disciples receive their glorified body and their sin nature is truly done away.

Participation in this feast requires enduring one week without sandwiches, burgers, pizza, pastries, and all other bread products. The health benefits are apparent too, as the Creator has built into His feasts an annual cleanse. What a wonderful way of honoring Messiah's selfless act as the Lamb of God who takes away the *leaven* of the world!

First-Fruits Sunday

The feast of First-Fruits always occurs on the first day of the week (Sunday) following Passover. While not a high Sabbath or holy convocation, it's an *Appointed Time* listed among them in the 23rd chapter of Leviticus:

> The LORD *spoke to Moses, "Tell the Israelis that when you enter the land that I'm about to give you and gather its produce, you are to bring <u>a sheaf from the first portion of your harvest to the priest, who will offer the sheaf in the LORD's presence for your acceptance. The priest is to wave it on the day after the Sabbath</u> ... You are not to eat bread, parched grain, or fresh grain until that day when you've brought the offering of your God. This is to be an eternal ordinance throughout your generations, wherever you live."*
> (Leviticus 23:9-11, 14; emphasis added)

On this First-fruits Sunday following Passover, the High Priest would take a premiere sheaf of the first-fruits barley- and wheat harvest and then elevate it, or wave it, before God in hopes of His acceptance. The shadow-picture in this pertains to the risen Messiah on Sunday following Passover ascending into heaven as the premiere glorified Man and being accepted by God as the first of the first-fruits of all who shall be raised from the dead and inherit a perfect, glorified body.

> *But now is Christ risen from the dead, [and] become the first-fruits of them that slept.*
> *(1 Corinthians 15:20)*

> *And He Christ is before all things, and by Him all things consist. And He is the head of the body, the church: who is the beginning, the firstborn from the dead; that in all [things] He might have the preeminence. For it pleased [the Father] that in Him should all fullness dwell. And, having made peace through the blood of the [stake], by Him to reconcile all things unto Himself; by Him [I say], whether [they be] things in earth or things in heaven.*
> *(Colossians 1:17-20, emphasis added)*

While First-fruits commemorates Messiah's resurrection and acceptance as the sheaf-offering, it has a yet future application [rehearsal], too. Upon Messiah's return, His disciples shall awaken in their graves, be changed in the twinkling of an eye, and be caught up with those still living to meet Jesus in the air whereupon they shall constitute the fullness of the First-fruits harvest:

> For the Lord Himself shall descend from heaven with a shout, with the voice of the archangel, and with the trump of God: and the dead in Christ shall rise first:
> (1 Thessalonians 4:16)

> These are they which were not defiled with women [spiritual whoring]; for they are [spiritual] virgins. These are they which follow the Lamb whithersoever He goeth. These were redeemed from among men, [being] the first-fruits unto God and to the Lamb. (Revelation 14:4)

Scripture addresses three phases of being born into eternity: 1) Messiah upon His resurrection is the first of the first-fruits, 2) those changed upon His Second Coming are the remainder of the first-fruits, and 3) the Great Harvest at the end of the age.

> But now is Christ risen from the dead, [and] become the first-fruits of them that slept. For since by man [came] death, by man [came] also the resurrection of the dead. For as in Adam all die, even so in Christ shall all be made alive. But every man in his own order:

> *Christ the first-fruits; afterward they that are*
> *Christ's at His [Second] coming. Then*
> *[cometh] the end... (1 Corinthians 15:20-24)*

Although there's no specific act involved in commemorating and rehearsing the feast of First-fruits, this is the occasion for which the disciples were gathered in the upper-room when Jesus appeared to them on Sunday evening following His resurrection. (A full accounting of the events of First-fruits is detailed in the follow-up book, *Messiah's Final 50 Days: An Alternate Chronology in Light of the Sign of Jonah.*)

But First-fruits Sunday does start the counting of the *omer* which culminates with the next *Appointed Time* known as "Pentecost" on the fiftieth day; when the Holy Spirit was poured out upon the earth:

> *Starting the day after the Sabbath [First-*
> *fruits Sunday], count for yourselves seven*
> *weeks from the day you brought the sheaf of*
> *wave offering. They are to be complete[,]*
> *count fifty days to the day[.] [A]fter the*
> *seventh Sabbath bring a new meal offering*
> *to the LORD. (Leviticus 23:15-16)*

It's important for there to be an accurate reckoning of First-fruits Sunday in order for there to be an accurate reckoning of the day of Pentecost. It's crucial that First-fruits be correctly commemorated / rehearsed on the Sunday following Passover (always between the 15th and 21st day in the month of the *Abib*). Remember, these are *feasts of the LORD*, and they must be reckoned according to His calendar; not according to man's calendar or man's tradition. Absurdly, Easter can occur before Passover (His resurrection before His death) and at other times as much as a month after Passover. When this is the case, it's clear indication that God's instructions as relayed through Moses are not being followed!

Spring Feasts Summary

The spring *feasts of the LORD* are perpetual holy days which commemorate the momentous events usurped by Good Friday and Easter Sunday. These are shadow-pictures and rehearsals revealed upon Mount Sinai in Arabia 1500 years before being fulfilled to the very day in the person of Jesus of Nazareth. These are God's *Appointed Times* which Jesus and the apostles observed throughout their entire lifetimes.

The Good Friday – Easter Sunday tradition was never observed by the apostles. Nowhere in Scripture is there reference to apostles commemorating Good Friday; nowhere in Scripture is there an example of Messianic believers participating in Easter morning festivities. The apostles all maintained the tradition of observing the *feasts of the LORD*, albeit in their Messianic context and without any imposed rabbinic regulations. To anyone doing otherwise, the apostles forewarned:

Therefore, brethren, stand fast, and hold [to] the traditions which ye have been taught, whether by word, or our epistle.
(2 Thessalonians 2:15)

Now we command you, brethren, in the name of our Lord Jesus Christ that ye withdraw yourselves from every brother that walketh disorderly, and not after the tradition which he received of us.
(2 Thessalonians 3:6)

Scriptural confirmation is the ultimate validation of truth. In the case of a Friday cruci-fiction, the result is clear: it fails miserably. God is worthy of so much more than this contrived remembrance of His ultimate gift to humanity.

Jesus entered into creation, tabernacle among men, offered Himself as the perfect sin-offering, and was successfully accepted by God the Father as the first of the First-fruits. These are the glorious, earth-shaking events which have changed the course of history, and in which a Christian's heart rejoices and longs to celebrate.

There's no disagreement as to the worthiness of the occasions, but as opposed to His sacrificial death as the Lamb of God being a footnote attributed to the Friday before Easter; instead of celebrating a counterfeit tradition imposed by the Catholic Church in the fourth-century; instead of one day of festivities of pagan origin encompassing a sunrise service, the coloring of eggs, prolific rabbits, and a ham dinner -- it's time to become reacquainted with the *feasts of the LORD* which have Godly history spanning 3500 years!

Think about it -- Moses, Joshua, King David, Solomon, the prophets Jonah, Jeremiah, Isaiah, and Daniel, as well as the New Covenant authors Matthew, Mark, Luke, John, Peter, Paul, and James. These are but the short-list of Biblical characters who honored and observed these *feasts of the LORD;* and, of course, the Master Himself – Jesus.

Granted, it's a new concept to most of the body-of-believers. It's a predicament reminiscent of the kingdom of Judah in the 7th century BCE. They, too, had become estranged from the *feasts of the LORD*. However, under King Josiah, when a scroll described as *'the book of the law of YHVH by the hand of Moses'* was found in a closet of the Temple Treasury, it was taken before the masses and read publicly so all would hear and comprehend the instructions of the Almighty.

The people thereafter repented of the false doctrines they inherited from their forefathers. They went out and destroyed the objects of worship dedicated to Baal, Ashtoreth, Chemosh, Topheth, Molech, *"and for all the [counterfeit] hosts of heaven."*[343] They executed the pagan priests, and in an extreme act of desecration they exhumed and burned the remains of their former pagan priests. Most importantly, they reinstituted the observance of Passover and the other *feasts of the LORD:*

---

[343] 2 Kings 23:4

And the king commanded all the people, saying, "Keep the Passover unto the LORD your God, as written in the book of this covenant." Surely there was not holden such a Passover from the days of the judges that judged Israel, nor in all the days of the kings of Israel, nor of the kings of Judah; But in the eighteenth year of king Josiah, [wherein] this Passover was holden to the LORD in Jerusalem. (2 Kings 23:21-23)

So in the spirit of King Josiah, prayerfully consider grounding yourself in Scripture with eight days of Biblical celebration in the same manner as Jesus and the early church. *"Therefore, let us keep the feast [of Unleavened Bread]"* by preparing on the Passover to commemorate Messiah's sacrificial death in *our* stead -- *"This do in remembrance of Me."*[344] Eliminate leavened products from *your* life for seven days in gratitude of having been forgiven, and in recognition of the call-to-action to stop willfully sinning. And finally rejoice on First-fruits Sunday in celebration of Messiah having been accepted by God the Father as the First-fruits sheaf-offering, and in anticipation of the completion of the First-fruits harvest at His Second Coming.

There's nothing pagan or legalistic or antiquated about keeping God's commands as set forth in the Books of Moses; it's just obedient immersion in the unadulterated Word of God as revealed through the hand of Moses, and exemplified in the life of our Savior -- Jesus the Christ.

---

[344] Luke 22:19

Chapter Nine
The Messianic Blueprint

Behold, I send you forth as sheep in the midst of wolves:
be ye therefore wise as serpents, and harmless as doves.
(Matthew 10:16)

The Dove and the Olive Branch

While the *sign of Jonah* clearly entails a literal three days and three nights, the Messianic typology within Jonah extends far beyond this aspect. As detailed in Chapter Five, the *Scroll of Jonah* allegorically foretells the plight of the Hebrew people from pre-Babylonian captivity to dispersement among the nations, and from their rejection of the *Oracles of God* to their enduring bitterness towards the Almighty for not destroying the Gentiles.

Yet more than this, the *Scroll of Jonah* proves to be the blueprint by which the Messiah patterned His earthly ministry. Jonah is the decoding manuscript by which to decipher several obscurities within Messiah's ministry. The evidence shows Jesus' entire ministry was predicated upon this Galilean prophet-of-old. At the same time, the precision with which Jesus' ministry incorporated all of the elements within Jonah's account equates to an almost incomprehensible adherence to Scriptural precedence as stipulated in Deuteronomy-13.

The prophet Jonah lived in the 8th century BCE during the reign of Jeroboam II; King of Samaria. He was the son of the prophet *Amittai* of *Gath-hepher*,[345] part of the northern Kingdom; most likely from the tribe of Zebulon.[346] *Gath-hepher* was a city near Nazareth, which means Jonah, like Jesus, came from Galilee.

Amittai, Jonah's father, means 'truth.' So Jonah was the 'son of truth' *(bar Amittai). Jonah* means 'dove,' which is a symbol of the Holy Spirit. The typology is captivating because Jesus was conceived through the Holy Spirit[347] and which came on Him as

a dove when He was baptized;[348] Himself being the Son of the Most High[349] who is *truth.*[350]

Mention of a dove first appears in Genesis 8:8 amid the great flood. After nine months aboard the ark, Noah sends forth a raven and then a dove. The raven flies to and fro, but the dove returns to him. A week later, Noah sends forth the dove again, and that evening it returns bearing an olive branch. Another week later, Noah sends forth the dove yet again but it doesn't return. Hence, the dove is the harbinger of good news, for it indicates Noah's family has been delivered from God's judgment upon the earth.

---

[345] Jonah 1:1; 2 Kings 14:25
[346] Joshua 19:10-16
[347] Matthew 1:18, Luke 1:35
[348] Luke 3:22, John 1:32
[349] Luke 1:32
[350] John 14:6

Likewise, Messiah is the harbinger of Good News; for His acceptance by the Almighty as the first-fruits sheaf-offering indicates those who are His will be delivered from God's judgment upon the earth at the end of the age.

Moreover, within this episode is an awesome shadow-picture: the *raven* represents the devil (Lucifer); the *dove* represents Jesus; the *ark* represents heaven; and *Noah* represents God the Father. It signifies that Lucifer was first given dominion over the earth but spent his time *"going to and fro"*[351] according to his own purpose. Jesus is subsequently sent forth whereupon He establishes the Melchezidek priesthood,[352] and then returns to the Heavenly Father. Jesus is sent forth again whereupon He incarnates as the Son of Man, dies for humanity's sins, arises the third day, and returns to the Father at evening[353] bearing a first-fruits offering -- an olive branch. Note that Jesus didn't deliver the entire olive tree nor even a sizable branch, but simply a first-fruits twig-sized offering. Lastly, Jesus is sent forth a third time but doesn't return, for at that time He reigns over His millennial kingdom.

This shadow-picture takes on additional depth with the fact doves and pigeons (of close relation) are the only birds suitable for sacrifice;[354] another subtle indicator pointing to Messiah's sacrificial death.

---

[351] Job 1:7 and 2:2
[352] Genesis 14:18
[353] Genesis 8:11, emphasis added
[354] Leviticus 1:14; 5:7; 12:6, 8; 14:22; see also Genesis 15:9-10

The dove was invoked by King David as an emblem of purity;[355] and by King Solomon as an emblem of endearment[356] and devoted affection.[357] The dove is also an emblem of love, hope, innocence, and peace. These are all traits encompassing the Messiah who is referred to as the *"prince of peace."*[358]

> *And, having made peace through the blood of His cross, by Him to reconcile all things unto Himself; by Him, I say, whether they be things in earth, or things in heaven.* (Colossians 1:20)

> *Therefore being justified by faith, we have peace with God through our Lord Jesus Christ.* (Romans 5:1)

> *For He is our peace, who hath made both one, and hath broken down the middle wall of partition between us.* (Ephesians 2:14)

> *...the gospel of peace.* (Ephesians 6:15)

In this context, the Holy Ghost descending upon Jesus as a dove when He was baptized in the Jordan River takes on extraordinary significance. It's indication that Jesus totally embodied the *sign of Jonah* (*dove*), and from that moment onward His works exemplified the *Scroll of Jonah*.

---

[355] Psalms 68:13
[356] Songs 4:1, 5:2, 5:12
[357] Songs 1:15; 2:14
[358] Isaiah 9:6

Precedence for Messiah's Ministry

In noting the remarkable similarities within their two ministries, the first point of interest is Jonah prophesying *'to the Jew first'* as seen in 2 Kings 14:25, but he goes on to share the Word of God with the Gentiles in Nineveh. Similarly, Jesus at first declares He has come *"only to the lost sheep of Israel,"*[359] but He goes on to commission His disciples to share the Gospel with the whole world:

> *He told them... that repentance and remission of sins should be preached in His name among all nations, beginning at Jerusalem. (Luke 24:46-47)*

The apostles were obedient to Jesus' command, and likewise preached *'to the Jew first'* in Jerusalem but they went on to carry the Gospel into every nation. They imitated *'to the Jew first'* as a pattern predicated by Jonah and emulated by Jesus:

> *Then Paul and Barnabas waxed bold, and said, "It was necessary that the Word of God should first have been spoken to you [children of Israel]: but seeing ye put it from you, and judge your-selves unworthy of everlasting life, lo, we turn to the Gentiles. For so hath the Lord commanded us, [saying], 'I have set thee to be a light of the Gentiles, that thou shouldest be for salvation unto the ends of the earth.'" (Acts 13:46-47)*

---

[359] Matthew 15:24

Jonah, however, wasn't excited about his commission to share the *Word of God* with the Gentiles, and hastily set sail in the opposite direction. God sent forth a mighty tempest to compel Jonah into obedience, but he retreated to the inner recesses of the ship and fell into a deep sleep. Jonah slept soundly through the tempest as the ship took on water and was about to break apart when he was awakened by a frantic captain and crew in fear for their lives. It's reminiscent of Jesus sleeping soundly through a storm on the Sea of Galilee as their vessel took on water and His disciples frantically awakened Him in fear for their lives.[360] In both cases, the seas were calmed and the experience led the crew into a personal relationship with the Creator of dry ground and sea.

It's a principle still applicable to this day: when aboard God's vessel, Noah's Ark being another example, the storms of life present no substantial danger. The faithful can sleep soundly knowing their circumstances are temporal; for even should injury or death occur, the Almighty will soon calm the seas of tribulation and tranquility will reign into eternity.

The intrinsic typology has a future application, too. When in the midst of tribulation, while the whole world trembles before a jealous and angry God, those who are His need not be fearful amid the carnage and chaos. The greatest tempest the world has ever known will soon be calmed, and the crew preserved through shall come to know their Heavenly Father in a capacity beyond anyone's current capability to comprehend.

---

[360] Mark 4:37-38; Luke 8:23-24

The mariners cast lots before Jonah in the same manner as the Roman soldiers cast lots before Jesus at the foot of the execution-stake.[361] When they determined Jonah to be the source of their woes, Jonah explained he was a prophet of God Almighty who hadn't wronged anyone, but was running away. After questioning him, the mariners deemed Jonah to be *"innocent blood;"*[362] just as after questioning Jesus, Pontius Pilate deemed Him to be *"innocent blood."*[363] Furthermore, just as the mariners didn't want to be accountable for Jonah's blood, so Pilate washed his hands of Jesus' blood.[364]

After the mariners prayed to God Almighty to be held blameless, they *"...took up Jonah, and cast him forth into the sea."*[365] The term "took up" is derived from the Hebrew word נשא or *nasa'* (Strong's H5375) which means 'to lift, bear up, carry.' It indicates Jonah was *lifted up* to be thrown overboard in the same manner as Jesus was *lifted up* to be crucified.

Reference to 'lifted up' has its origins in the brass serpent upon a pole which Moses *lifted up* before the people whereupon anyone who'd been bitten by a serpent would be healed and live.[366] The serpent is symbolic of sin while brass is symbolic of judgment; therefore, the brass serpent symbolizes 'sin judged.' In this context Jesus foretold He'd be *lifted up*:

---

[361] See Jonah 1:7 and John 19:24
[362] Jonah 1:14
[363] Matthew 27:4; see also John 18:38
[364] Matthew 27:24
[365] Jonah 1:15
[366] Numbers 21:7

> *And as Moses lifted up the serpent in the*
> *wilderness, even so must the Son of Man be*
> *lifted up: that whosoever believeth in Him*
> *should not perish, but have eternal life.*
> *(John 3:14-15)*

> *"And I, if I be lifted up from the earth, will draw*
> *all men unto Me." This He said, signifying what*
> *death He should die. (John 12:32-33)*

As Jonah was *lifted up* by Gentile mariners in the course of casting him into the sea, so Jesus was *lifted up* by Gentile Romans in the course of raising the execution-stake (pole).

Both instances constitute a sacrifice: Jonah's life to save the mariners, and Jesus' life to save the world. Noteworthy is that both sacrifices were performed by Gentiles; not Levite priests. In the case of the mariners, the experience was so stirring that they believed in God Almighty and thereafter came to salvation. In the case of the Roman executioners, particularly the centurion who realized *"Truly this man was the Son of God,"*[367] typology suggests they, too, believed in God Almighty and thereafter came to salvation.

Jonah embraced his death as a prophet of God, and willingly allowed the mariners to cast him into the sea. In like manner, Jesus embraced His death as the Passover Lamb of God, and

---

[367] Mark 15:39

was silent[368] in allowing the Romans to scourge His flesh and nail Him to the execution-stake.

> *He did not open His mouth; like a lamb that is led to slaughter, and like a sheep that is silent before its shearers, so He did not open His mouth. (Isaiah 53:7)*

Echoing another Messianic prophecy within the *Scroll of Isaiah*, the mariners prayed to God Almighty, saying: *"for Thou, O LORD, hast done as It pleased Thee."*[369] In terms of Jesus' sacrificial death, Isaiah says:

> *The LORD was pleased to crush Him, putting Him to grief, if He would render Himself as a guilt offering... (Isaiah 53:10, emphasis added)*

In an unexpected turn of events, Jonah was swallowed by a great fish, taken down into the abyss, and out of sight of the Almighty from where he cried out: *"...I am cast out of Thy sight..."*[370] In like manner, Jesus cried out from the execution-stake, *"My God, My God, why hast Thou forsaken Me?"*[371]

While confined in the belly of the great fish, a crown of seaweed wrapped around Jonah's head as a crown of thorns

---

[368] Matthew 27:12-19
[369] Jonah 1:14, emphasis added
[370] Jonah 2:4
[371] Matthew 27:46; see also Psalms 22:1

would wrap around Messiah's head.[372] Therein, *"...the floods compassed [Jonah] about: all Thy billows and Thy waves passed over [him]..."*[373]

The word translated "waves" is derived from the Hebrew word גּל or *gal* (Strong's #H1530); meaning 'heap, spring, wave, billow.' It stems from a root word meaning 'to roll, roll away, roll down, roll together.' A *gal* of water (rolling water) is a 'wave,' and a *gal* of stones is a 'heap' or 'pile' of stones.

A heap of stones was customarily piled upon the bodies of the dead if they weren't entombed. As an example, upon the death of King David's son, Absalom, Scripture records:

> *And ten young men that bare Joab's armour compassed about and smote Absalom, and slew him... And they took Absalom, and cast him into a great pit in the wood, and laid a very great heap of stones upon him.*
> *(2 Samuel 18:15 & 17, emphasis added)*

The imagery portrayed in the *Scroll of Jonah*, which is much more evident in Hebrew, is that of death and burial. Just as Jonah was inside the great fish in the abyss of the sea with waves that rolled over him in figurative death, so Jesus was buried in the heart of the earth with a stone rolled over His tomb in literal death.

---

[372] Jonah 2:5
[373] Jonah 2:3

While sloshing around inside the belly of the great fish, Jonah repented of his disobedience. God then caused the great fish to vomit Jonah out upon dry ground. Yet, as a consequence of 72-hours in gastric acid, Jonah emerged without any remaining skin pigmentation; i.e. bleached white. Just as Jonah was physically changed when he emerged from the belly of the great fish, so Jesus was physically changed -- glorified -- when He emerged from the heart of the earth!

Ministries of Repentance

After repenting and being vomited out upon dry ground, Jonah obediently journeyed to Nineveh to warn the citizenry of their impending judgment. So it was that after three days and three nights in the belly of the great fish, Jonah emerged to preach throughout the city of Nineveh forewarning 40 days:

> And Jonah began to enter into the city a day's journey, and he cried, and said, 'Yet forty days, and Nineveh shall be overthrown.' (Jonah 3:4)

In like manner, after three days and three nights in the heart of the earth, Jesus emerged to preach throughout the land of Judah forewarning 40 days:

> To whom also He shewed Himself alive after His passion by many infallible proofs, being seen of them forty days, and speaking of the things pertaining to the kingdom of God. (Acts 1:3)

235

Moreover, at the end of forty days, Jonah was found to the east of Nineveh[374] whereupon the narrative abruptly stops. Just as at the end of forty days, Jesus was found east of Jerusalem -- on the Mount of Olives -- whereupon He ascends and the Gospel narratives abruptly stop!

The Ninevites received Jonah and repented, and thereby God relented of the punishment He threatened. In like manner, if the inhabitants of this world will receive Jesus as their Savior and repent of their evil ways, then His sacrificial death will be substituted in their stead and God will again relent from the punishment He has threatened.

The Ninevites serve as a powerful demonstration of God's desire for all people to heed the warning, repent of their sins, and seek forgiveness through the power of Jesus' blood in order that they, too, can be spared everlasting destruction.

Repentance is a major theme of both ministries, so it's not surprising to find a shadow-picture corresponding to baptism in the *Scroll of Jonah*: a rebellious sinner living a life  away from God who is immersed into the sea and arises a new man obedient to God's commands.

---

[374] Jonah 4:4

In this sense, everyone can be seen as a type of Jonah. All have lived a life away from God and disobedient to His calling, yet all are given the opportunity to repent, to be immersed for the remission of sins, and to go forth into all the world sharing the Gospel with every man and woman. The God of Heaven is merciful to all who believe and keep His commandments.

The Great Commission hasn't changed from times of antiquity until now. Just as Israel-of-old was commissioned to be a light unto the Gentiles[375] -- Jonah's manifest obedience being an allegorical fulfillment -- so Jesus renewed that commission In the New Covenant:

> Go ye therefore, and teach all nations, baptizing
> them in the name of the Father, and of the Son,
> and of the Holy Ghost: teaching them to observe
> all things whatsoever I have commanded you.
> (Matthew 28:19-20)

So be vigilant in not being as the Israelites-of-old -- stubborn, disobedient, and backslidden -- but be faithful in disseminating the *good news* at home and abroad. The last time Messiah came to serve, and the next time He's coming to judge. Therefore, turn from your evil ways and confess Jesus as Savior, and in return He shall bestow upon you the crown of life![376]

---

[375] Isaiah 49:6
[376] James 1:12

In regards to that future judgment, referred to in Scripture as *the Last Great Day*, Jesus foretold:

> *The men of Nineveh shall rise in judgment with*
> *this generation, and shall condemn it: because*
> *they repented at the preaching of Jonah; and,*
> *behold, a greater than Jonah is here.*
> *(Matthew 12:41)*

Jesus informed the Pharisees their unbelief was culpable given the Ninevites' change of heart with far less evidence. Other than his unsettling appearance, Jonah's message lacked signs and wonders; and yet the Ninevites recognized its divine origin and responded with genuine repentance. On the other hand, Jesus' message was accompanied by spectacular miracles including the restoration of sight to a man born blind and the raising of the dead; and yet the Pharisees' hearts were hardened to the point that witnessing prophecy fulfilled wasn't enough to persuade them.

The generation in which Messiah lived stands condemned, but this generation hangs in the balance. Will it heed the warning to throw off the pagan and centuries-old traditions which fly in the face of Scriptural truths, or will they be like the Pharisees who hardened their hearts in order to continue doing that which is comfortable? Will they be persuaded by spectacular Biblical evidences reproving the events of Holy Week to have occurred on God's calendar and according to His *Appointed Times*, or will they cling to a corrupted belief-system handed down to them through their forefathers?

...the Gentiles shall come unto Thee from the ends of the earth, and shall say, "Surely our fathers have inherited lies, vanity, and [things] wherein [there is] no profit." (Jeremiah 16:19)

In comparing *"Nineveh, that great city,"*[377] with Jerusalem, the other *"great city,"*[378] history records the Assyrian capital to be an architectural wonder yet morally depraved and steeped in the worship of *Ishtar*. At the same time, Hebrew prophets declared Judah's capital to be a spiritual harlot[379] and the equivalent of Sodom and Gomorrah.[380]

Nevertheless, the two great cities ultimately differed in that the Ninevites welcomed the Word of God and in so doing prolonged Nineveh's longevity, while the Judeans expelled the Word of God and in so doing sealed Jerusalem's fate:

And it came to pass, that, when I [Paul] was come again to Jerusalem, even while I prayed in the Temple, I was in a trance; And saw Him saying unto me, "Make haste, and get thee quickly out of Jerusalem: <u>for they will not receive thy testimony concerning Me.</u>"
(Acts 22:17-18, emphasis added)

---

[377] Jonah 3:2
[378] Revelation 11:8
[379] Isaiah 1:21
[380] Isaiah 1:10

Ironically, the city of Nineveh -- not Jerusalem -- proves to be an example of a generation repenting of personal and national sin. The Ninevites constitute the precedent of a generation discarding their evil ways and inscribing God's perfect *Law* upon their hearts. To do likewise is to inherit eternal life and potentially reign alongside Messiah in His Millennial Kingdom;[381] to fail to do so is to risk hearing Messiah profess on that Last Great Day:

> And then will I profess unto them, "I never knew you: depart from Me, ye that work iniquity [contrary to God's Law]." (Revelation 20:4)

Forty: Testing and Probationary Period

As Jonah's forewarned destruction of Nineveh followed forty days, so Jesus' prophesized destruction of Jerusalem followed forty 'prophetic days' (forty years) with its bloody fate coming to pass in the autumn of 70 CE.

When implementing the Biblical day-for-a-year principle and multiplying each year by God's 360-day calendar, forty prophetic years equates to 14,400 days (40 x 360). Therefore, the nation of Judah was allotted 14,400 days to either open their hearts and minds to Jesus of Nazareth being the Anointed One of the Most High, or else be doomed to national destruction.

---

[381] Revelation 20:4

Starting upon the high Sabbath concluding the Feast of Unleavened Bread (21st day in the month of the *Abib*) in 31 CE whereupon everyone gave glory to God Almighty before heading home, Judah had exactly 14,400 days to contemplate the surreal events that transpired amid that year's festival: Jesus' Triumphal Entry, His sudden and revolting crucifixion on the Passover, His claim that He'd arise again on the third day, the empty tomb, and His disciples' testimony that He'd appeared to them on the Feast of First-fruits.

Towards the end of their 40-year probationary period, on the 9th of *Av* (August 4th or 5th) in 70 CE, Jesus' words concerning the destruction of the Temple came to pass as a consequence of not knowing Daniel's 70-week prophecy pointing to His public appearance on the 10th of *Abib* in 31 CE. At the same time, its destruction should've served as a major point of reconsideration because the people knew the Messiah had been prophesized to enter into the second Temple;[382] therefore, upon its destruction, reality should've set in that Messiah must've already been there!

The nation should've realized that Jesus of Nazareth, as an only viable option, is the Messiah; and that His disciples' witness is true! But they refused to believe even to the point of thinking God's Word had been broken. Alas, two months later, on the Day of Atonement (10th day of *Tishri*) in 70 CE, their 14,400-day probation period expired and the unbelieving nation's destruction became a foregone conclusion.

---

[382] Haggai 2:2-9

Calculations: from 31 CE to 70 CE is 39 years; multiplying 39 years by 365 days (solar calendar year) equates to 14,235; adding 10 days for leap years (32-, 36-, 40-, 44-, 48-, 52-, 56-, 60-, 64-, and 68 CE) totals 14,245; and, finally, adding 155 calendar days (May 2nd to Oct 3rd) sums up to 14,400.

Judah's 40-Year Probation Period

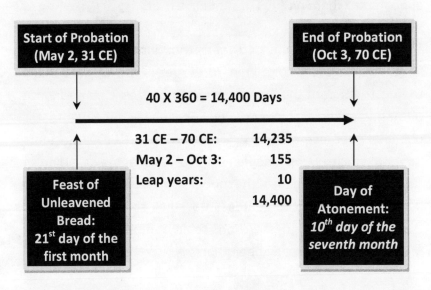

The Day of Atonement -- the most holy day of the year when miraculous signs had historically indicated whether national atonement was accepted or rejected -- is the very day upon which Judah's probation period ended, and the nation was judged to be unworthy of atonement and sentenced to desolation.

The outcome was tragic, but ultimately not surprising; for Judah's rejection of Messiah as well as its desolation is fully predicated in the *Scroll of Jonah*. Foremost, Jonah being rejected by his own countrymen is a shadow-picture of Messiah being rejected by His own countrymen.

Yet deeper within Jonah typology is something even more profound: after begrudgingly warning the Ninevites of God's impending judgment, Jonah tabernacled in the heat outside of the city in hopes of seeing it destroyed. As Jonah waited, God prepared a gourd (symbolic of the Promised Land) to relieve him of his grief. But God also prepared a worm, תּוֹלָע or *towla`* (Strong #H8438), to smite the gourd and make it wither. What is the symbolism of this worm?

Recall the words that Messiah uttered while hanging upon the execution-stake as foretold in the *Scroll of Psalms*:

> *"But I [am] a <u>worm</u> [תּוֹלָע or towla`], and no man;*
> *a reproach of men, and despised of the people."*
> *(Psalms 22:6, emphasis added)*

Yes, the bloody Scarlet Worm who attaches Himself to a branch and dies so that others may live, is the same worm that God prepared to destroy the gourd and make it wither! The Passover Lamb of God who takes away the sins of the world, is the One who exiled the Hebrews from the Promised Land and caused it to lie barren due to Judah's failure to acknowledge Him as Messiah and uphold God's commands by the end of their 40 years of testing!

In like manner as Judah was given forty prophetic years of testing/probation, the Church will endure forty Jubilee years[383] of testing/probation; (40 x 50), i.e. 2000 years. This is seen in the shadow-picture of Jesus residing among the Samaritans for *"two days."*[384] The Bible portrays the history of the world -- Adam through the Great White Throne Judgment[385] -- as being 7000 years; with the Sabbath millennium being Messiah's reign upon the earth. Therefore, with *"one day is with the LORD as a thousand years,"*[386] world history is figuratively expressed in the 7-day week.

For instance, God created the lights in the heavens on the fourth day,[387] and Jesus -- the light of the world[388] -- was born in the fourth millennium. In this sense, Jesus' *"two days"* among the Samaritans after being unwelcomed in Judea correlates to the Word of God residing 2000 years among the Gentiles after being rejected by Judah.

Consider also Hosea 6:2 -- *"After two days will He revive us: in the third day He will raise us up, and we shall live in His sight."* This implies that after nearly 2000 years of desolation, Messiah will return to revive Israel; then in the subsequent 1000-year period (the Sabbath millennium), His faithful servants will be raised up from the dead to live and reside in His presence as He reigns from His millennial throne in Jerusalem.

---

[383] Leviticus 25:8-12
[384] John 4:40-43
[305] Revelation 20:11
[386] 2 Peter 3:8
[387] Genesis 1:14-19
[388] John 8:12

Certainly this begs the question: what triggered the start of the forty cycles of Jubilee years which constitute the Church Age? Was it Jesus' baptism in late 29- or early 30 CE, or the pouring out of the Holy Spirit at Pentecost in the spring of 31 CE? Was it the start of the rejected atonement sacrifices in the autumn of 30 CE, or the end of Judah's probationary period in the autumn of 70 CE? No matter the answer, the end of the age is imminent and Messiah's return looms in the very near future!

In drawing to a close, hopefully some of the depth and complexity in the *Scroll of Jonah* will challenge the Christian pulpits to re-assess their take on the Galilean prophet-of-old. While the most disobedient prophet, Jonah is also the most misunderstood prophet; just as Messiah was misunderstood in His First Coming. Jesus hadn't come to rule as the *Lion of the tribe of Judah*, but He'd come to serve and to ultimately die on behalf of humanity as the *Passover Lamb of God*.

The prophet Jonah is misunderstood because his disobedience was not out of pride, but out of love. Jonah foresaw Israel's fate should the Ninevites repent, and chose to die rather than subject them to the afflictions of their enemy.

In this sense, the Messianic implication of Jonah is striking: Jonah, in disobedience, sacrificed himself out of love for his people, and ended up in the belly of the great fish for three days and three nights; Jesus, in perfect obedience, sacrificed Himself out of love for His people, and ended up in the heart of the earth for three days and three nights.

Both Jonah and Jesus sought to substitute his own life for the preservation of Israel. Jonah sought temporal salvation in destroying Israel's mortal enemies while Jesus sought eternal salvation in destroying Israel's spiritual enemy. Jonah failed in his short-sighted attempt, and yet Messiah was decisively victorious.

This is exemplified like no other in the fact Jonah's tomb, reputedly in a village near Jaffa, Joppa, remains occupied while Jesus' tomb in Jerusalem remains empty!

Reputedly Jonah's Ossuary near Jaffa, Joppa

Conclusion

When reflecting upon the all-encompassing *sign of Jonah*, Jesus is found to have meticulously fulfilled every facet. In terms of His three days and three nights in the heart of the earth, the apostle Paul confirmed *"...Jesus rose again the third day according to the Scriptures."*[389] Jesus was not raised contrary to Scripture, contrary to Jonah, nor contrary to His Word. God is not flattered by the rewriting of Biblical History. God is not appreciative of man made traditions which imply He is a liar.

---

[389] 1 Corinthians 15:4

The harmony of Scripture as an integrated whole proclaims Jesus to have been crucified Wednesday afternoon, buried that evening upon the mingling of days when the high Sabbath was beginning, and gloriously resurrected Saturday evening. Yet the days themselves are not what are important, but rather the duration of time He was dead and buried.

Beyond its 72-hour implication, Jesus remained entombed for precisely three days as defined in Genesis: *"And the evening and the morning were the first day... And the evening and the morning were the second day... And the evening and the morning were the third day."*[390] There are no partial days in this equation. Thursday evening and morning was the first day; Friday evening and morning was the second day; and Saturday evening and morning was the third day. It equates to *"three days and three nights"* is in its absolute most literal capacity.

This Scriptural certainty is not contingent upon His crucifixion being dated to 31 CE, nor His ministry entailing 13- to 19 months. Whatever opposing views people hold, and whatever dating revelations come, Messiah's *"three days and three nights in the heart of the earth"* will forever stand as a testament to His fulfillment of the *sign of Jonah*.

Jesus' Wednesday crucifixion and Saturday resurrection is a foundational tenet of Messianic understanding. Yet neither apostolic teaching nor example dictates the days of the week ought to be commemorated. They are merely historical record

---

[390] Genesis 1:5-13

in documenting that Jesus fulfilled the sign given as proof of His authority.

However, in recognition of the historical record, believers need to seriously reassess the repercussions of Good Friday – Easter Sunday before again passing it on to future generations. It's time for believers to reject this heresy outright. It's time to discard the worthless teachings of our youth, repent of our ignorance, and acknowledge *"Surely our fathers have inherited lies..."*[391]

God called His people out of Egypt 3500 years ago just as God calls His people out of spiritual Egypt today. Leave the false traditions and idolatrous customs of those harlot belief-systems behind, and *"Come out of her, My people!"*[392]

Instead of Good Friday – Easter Sunday, Jesus' disciples ought to be rejoicing in the Messianic significance of the *feasts of the LORD* which have pointed to His death and resurrection all along.

The prophet Jeremiah's words are just as applicable today as they were when first spoken:

> *Stand in the LORD's ways and see, and ask for the*
> *old paths where the good way is, and walk in it;*
> *Then you will find rest for your souls...*
> *(Jeremiah 6:16)*

---

[391] Jeremiah 16:19
[392] Revelation 18:4

Keep the feast of Passover and Unleavened Bread on the Biblically correct dates. Celebrate the feast of First-fruits when the resurrected Savior ascended into heaven and was accepted by God the Father as the worthy first-fruits sheaf-offering on behalf of all mankind!

Remember, the prophet Daniel forewarned: *"And he [Satan's religious hierarchy] shall speak [great] words against the most High, and shall wear out the saints of the most High, and think to change times and laws..."*[393] This inherently includes the changing of God's *Appointed Times*. Daniel's dire warning has tragically come to pass -- Passover has been changed to Good Friday, and First-fruits has been changed to Easter Sunday -- yet so much of the Christian world remains oblivious to this critical fact.

Make no mistake, a major reason the Hebrew people oppose the idea of Jesus being the Messiah is because of customs like Easter which are steeped in paganism. Jews, by way of Christians, believe Jesus is the progenitor of Easter, and yet know the true Messiah would never condone such practices. Eggs are a pagan symbol of new life, rabbits are a prolific symbol of fertility, *Easter* itself is a thinly veiled reference to the bare-breasted goddess of fertility, and ham consumed at supper has direct correlation to worship of *Tammuz*.[394] The covenant people reason that the Man at the center of such pagan festivities cannot be the Messiah of Scripture; and consequently reject Him without further contemplation.

---

[393] Daniel 7:25, emphasis added
[394] See Ezekiel 8:13-14

On the other hand, if His disciples were to acknowledge and celebrate the *feasts of the LORD*, the Jews would immediately take notice. Their interest would be piqued as to why Gentiles are worshipping the God of Abraham, Isaac, and Jacob. And they would begin to search the Scriptures in order to learn whether these things concerning Jesus are true.

The apostle Paul relayed this to be the very reason salvation had come upon the Gentiles in the first place:

> *I say then, 'Have [Hebrews] stumbled that they should fall? God forbid! But [rather] through their fall, salvation [is come] unto the Gentiles, to provoke them [Hebrews] to jealousy.'* (Romans 11:11)

If Christians return to the Scriptural origins of their faith, and throw off the chains of pagan bondage which have weighed upon them so long that it seems the norm, then the Jews shall be provoked to jealousy. As a result, they will likewise undergo a revival, they too will begin to throw off their chains of *Talmudic* bondage, and they'll inevitably come to believe and accept Jesus as their personal Savior. Without a doubt, it'll be the greatest conversion of Hebrew brethren into Messianic believers the world has ever known!

Toward the end of two millennia, it's time for Jew and Gentile alike to become enlightened as to every aspect of Messiah's miraculous fulfillment of the *sign of Jonah*. The days until His return are few, so urgently go out and proclaim this *good news*!

ABIB 31 C.E.

Sun	Mon	Tues	Wed	Thur	Fri	Sabbath
				1 New Year	2	3
4	5	6	7	8	9	10 Triumphal Entry
11	12	13	14 Passover: Crucifixion	15 Unleavened Bread: High Sabbath	16	17 Resurrection
18 Feast of First-fruits	19	20	21 High Sabbath	22	23	24
25	26	27	28	29	30	

APPENDIX

A Brief History of Church Persecution

In the earliest days of the Christendom, a controversial and bloody dispute of unimaginable proportions erupted over the observance of Passover versus Easter. Over a million Messianic disciples were slain as a result of this controversy, yet today most Christians are oblivious to this part of Church history. Nevertheless, what proved to be an irreconcilable difference between the faithful followers of Jesus and the domineering Church in Rome was originally known as the *Quartodeciman Controversy*. This forsaken struggle for power and control spanned the first three centuries of the New Covenant era, but has also been revisited by numerous groups amid the past two millennia with limited degrees of success.

The premise of the controversy arose in the first-century while the apostles were still alive. Ancient rituals associated with the goddess *Ishtar* began to resurface mingled within the practices of church congregations. The apostles warned against it, and most believers heeded their warnings to steer clear. The first-century churches -- those found in the pages of the New Testament -- refrained from mingling pagan customs with the oracles of God. As a result, first-century Christians continued to observe Passover on the fourteenth day in the month of the *Abib* in the same manner Messiah delivered it to the apostles, and in the same manner the apostles delivered it to the next generation of disciples.[395]

However, after the deaths of the apostles, factions within the body of believers began to jostle for positions of power. Wolves in sheep's clothing began making self-serving claims of doctrinal changes. In particular, the Church in Rome discovered that "Christianizing" pagan customs greatly increased the attendance at worship services. As a result, the church in Rome began to rapidly grow in size while their teachings rapidly grew in popularity.

Emperor Constantine, in the fourth-century, would later capitalize on this amalgamation of religions when making Christianity the official state-religion. The idea of an Easter celebration greatly appealed to Gentile converts in that the mixing of paganism with the Christian celebrations made conversion easier.

In addition to the induction of fertility symbols, the Church in Rome sought to change the days of observance. Instead of commemorating the crucifixion on the fourteenth day in the month of the *Abib*, their doctrine associated the Friday before Easter (*Ishtar*) as the day of the crucifixion irrespective of the day of the month. The fundamental Christians strongly opposed the change, but as the number of Gentile Christians increased, so did the popularity of Easter; and as the popularity of Easter increased, so did the division within the churches.

---

[395] *The Two Babylons*, pp. 103-104

Polycarp: Disciple of the Apostle Yochanan

In the mid-second century, a man named *Polycarp* -- a direct disciple of John the Revelator -- was bishop of Smyrna. He held to the observance of Passover exactly as he received it from the beloved apostle. In the year 159 CE, Polycarp traveled to Rome to discuss with Anicetus, bishop of Rome (157-168), the significance of Passover in the course of urging Anicetus to reject the pagan celebration of Easter.

Polycarp explained that Passover was to be kept at evening on the fourteenth day in the month of the *Abib* in the same manner which Messiah instituted it during the Last Supper. Yet in spite of conversing with the man who learned the observance directly from the apostle who leaned upon the Master's bosom during the Last Supper, Anicetus was not persuaded that Passover should any longer be honored as the genuine commemoration of Messiah's death.

> "But Polycarp also was not only instructed by the apostles, and conversed with many who had seen Christ, but was also, by apostles in Asia, appointed bishop of the Church of Smyrna... He it was who, coming to Rome in the time of Anicetus, caused many to turn away from the... [celebration of Easter and return to the observance of Passover], proclaiming that he had received this one and sole truth from the apostles... While at Rome, Polycarp discussed with the Roman bishop the matter of the

255

introduction of the pagan Easter in place of the Passover... neither could Anicetus persuade Polycarp not to observe it because he had always observed it with John the Disciple of our Lord and the rest of the apostles with whom he associated; and neither did Polycarp persuade Anicetus to observe it, who said that he was bound to follow the customs of the presbyters before him."

(Ecclesiastical History, Book V, Ch. 24, in the "Nicene and Post-Nicene Fathers," Vol. 1)

Polycrates: Disciple of Polycarp

Asia Minor is where the apostle Paul spent most of his time, and where the apostle John spent his last days prior to being imprisoned on the Island of Patmos. Therefore, it's not surprising that the churches of Asia Minor are where Christians were most adamant about retaining the Gospel exactly as they'd been taught.

In the late second-century, the bishops of Asia Minor, led by a man named *Polycrates*, retained the observance of Passover as handed down to them through Polycarp. Distressed by the prevailing customs of the Church in Rome, they sought to again open a line of communication and re-address the Scriptural basis for commemorating the Passover in its Messianic context.

In 197 CE, Polycrates sent a letter to Victor, bishop of Rome (186-197), reiterating this long-held position:

> As for us, then, we scrupulously observe the exact day, neither adding nor taking away. For in Asia also great luminaries have fallen sleep, who shall rise again in the day of the Lord's coming, when He shall come with glory from heaven, and seek out all the saints. Among these are Philip, one of the twelve apostles, who fell asleep in Hierapolis; ... and, moreover, John, who was both a witness and a teacher, who reclined on the bosom of the Lord, and, being a priest, wore the sacerdotal plate. He fell asleep at Ephesus. And there is Polycarp in Smyrna, who was a bishop and a martyr... All these observed the fourteenth day of the Passover according to the Gospel, deviating in no respect, but following the rule of faith... For seven of my relatives were Bishops; and I am the eighth. And my relatives always observed the day when the people put away the leaven. I, therefore, ... have met with the brethren throughout the world, and have gone through every Holy Scripture, am not affrighted by terrifying words. For those greater than I have said 'We ought to obey God rather than man'...
>
> (Eusebius, *Church History*, Book V, Ch. 24)

This correspondence didn't resonate with the Roman bishop. Good Friday – Easter Sunday was the tradition prevailing in Rome at the time, and Victor demanded everyone throughout the empire likewise celebrate it. Polycrates and the other bishops of Asia Minor objected, and supported their stance with Scriptural evidences and historical precedent. Victor was incredulous, and angered to the point of excommunicating Polycrates and all the bishops who sided with him; though he was restrained from actually enforcing the decree of excommunication.

Easter Becomes Official Doctrine

A final settlement of the dispute was one among several reasons Emperor Constantine summoned the Council to Nicaea in 325 CE. After discussing the controversy, the Nicaean Council voted unanimously in favor of Easter and declared it was to be celebrated on the same day throughout the world.

After the Council adjourned, Emperor Constantine sent the following notice to all of the churches under his rule:

> At this meeting the question concerning the most holy day of Easter was discussed... Let us then have nothing in common with the Jews... It has been determined by the common judgment of all, that the... feast of Easter should be kept by all and in every place on one and the same day.
> (Eusebius, *Life of Constantine*, Book III, Ch. 66)

The reality of the matter is that the members of the Nicaean Council so abhorred the Jews and their customs that they disregarded the *Feasts of the LORD* simply because the Jews observed them; regardless of the Jews failure as a whole to comprehend the Messianic significance in the feasts. This anti-Semitism is further evidenced by the Council's ruling that the date of Easter could never coincide with Passover. In the event Easter Sunday occurred on the fourteenth day of the first month, then the festival of Easter was to be postponed until the following Sunday.[396]

> "And first of all, it appeared an unworthy thing that in the celebration of this most holy feast we should follow the practice of the Jews, who have impiously defiled their hands with enormous sin, and are, therefore, deservedly afflicted with blindness of soul. For we have it in our power, if we abandon their custom, to prolong the due observation of this ordinance to future ages, by a truer order, which we have preserved from the very day of the passion until the present time. Let us have nothing in common with the detestable Jewish crowd; for we have received from our Savior a different way."
>
> (Eusebius, *Life of Constantine*, Book III, Ch. 18)

Of course, not everyone agreed with the racist decrees of the Nicaean Council, nor did everyone readily accept the contrived reckoning for the date of Messiah's resurrection (the first Sunday after the first full moon following the spring equinox).

---

[396] Burns' *"The Council of Nicea,"* p. 46.

Many within the churches of Asia Minor planned to disregard the decision as to Good Friday – Easter Sunday and retain the apostolic tradition which stipulates observance on the same day as the Hebrews sacrificed the Passover lamb.

When Emperor Constantine became aware of their disregard for his ruling, he was enraged to the point of wanting to permanently extinguish any Passover observance. Emperor Constantine warned them in this official letter:

"To speak of your criminality as it deserves demands more time and leisure than I can give... Forasmuch, then, as it is no longer possible to bear with your pernicious errors, we give warning by this present statute that none of you henceforth presume to assemble yourselves together. We have directed, accordingly, that you be deprived of all the houses in which you are accustomed to hold your assemblies: and forbid the holding of your superstitious and senseless meetings, not in public merely, but in any private house or place whatsoever... and that these be made over without delay to the Catholic Church; that any other places be confiscated to the public service, and no facility whatsoever be left for any future gathering, in order that from this day forward none of your unlawful assemblies may presume to appear in any public or private place. Let this edict be made public..."
(*Life of Constantine*, Book III, Ch. 66)

To the dismay of the Messianic disciples in Asia Minor, the feast of Easter became the Church's official doctrine in 325 CE. They had fought long and hard against its acceptance, firmly believing the churches should hold to the observance of Passover, the Feast of Unleavened Bread, and First-fruits. Though many knew the new doctrine to be false, few were willing to separate themselves in accordance with Scripture. From this point onward, only a remnant held strong to the teachings of the apostles in spite of the persecution inflicted by a now powerful Church entity.

Persecution Intensifies

Emperor Constantine soon began a relentless campaign of persecution directed towards anyone unwilling to conform to the practices of the Catholic Church. Everyone was forced to either celebrate Easter or flee from the major cities and territories of the Roman Empire. Much of the remnant headed into the surrounding mountains and valleys, and eventually found refuge in what is now Armenia. They were known as *Quartodecimani*; from a Latin word meaning 'fourteeners.'

For the next several centuries, Catholic writers mention remnants of *Quartodecimani* within the bounds of the Roman Empire. As late as the fifth-century in Asia Minor, the bishop Chrysostom is known to have despised members of his Church who left in order to join the *Quartodecimans*.[397]

---

[397] Karl Baus' *"From the Apostolic Community to Constantine"*, pp. 271-272

The Paulicians

Continuing into the fifth and sixth centuries CE, the *Quartodecimani* were outcasts who lived in relative obscurity and largely kept to themselves. In addition to Armenia, many came to dwell in the remote mountains of modern-day Turkey where they co-existed peacefully with Muslim communities.

> "It was a huge recess or circular dam formed by the Taurus mountain range that furnished a comparatively secure abiding place for this ancient form of Christianity."
> (Karl Baus, *From the Apostolic Community to Constantine*, pp. 271-272)

In or around 657 CE, God raised up from among the remnant a man to revitalize the movement. In the town of *Mananeli*, a man named Constantine welcomed into his home a returning resident who had been held captive in Syria. Somewhere amid his journey, the returning resident obtained manuscripts of several New Covenant writings. Constantine was intrigued, and the man entrusted them to Constantine who then began studying, applying their teachings in his daily life, and preaching the *Good News* to others.

Constantine and his converts took on historical names. Constantine changed his name to *Silvanus*, after one of the apostle Paul's disciples. The assembly called themselves 'Paulicians;' likely after the apostle Paul but possibly after Paul of Samosata, a third-century bishop of Antioch who originated from a nearby community. The Paulicians founded their first community at *Kibossa*, Armenia.

Over the course of thirty years, Constantine-Silvanus led tens of thousands of people to faith in Jesus the Messiah. As the Paulicians grew in numbers and their teachings spread eastward across the Byzantine Empire, it caught the attention of the Byzantine emperor. In 684 CE, *Emperor Constantine Pogonatus* (668-685) commissioned an officer by the name of Simeon to quell the movement.

Simeon tracked down Constantine-Silvanus and other members, and under penalty of death ordered the assembly to cast stones at Constantine-Silvanus. A young man by the name of Justus, whom Constantine-Silvanus had adopted as a youth, cast his stone and as a result Constantine-Silvanus died, but as a whole the assembly held their stones. In a twist of fate, Simeon was so moved by the faith of Constantine-Silvanus and the others that Simeon himself became a believer.

Much like the apostle Paul, Simeon embraced the doctrine he was sent to stamp out. Simeon would later renounce his former life, his honors, and his wealth. He accepted Jesus as his personal Savior, changed his name per the custom of the Paulicians -- taking the name *Titus* -- and thereafter became a leader among the outcast community. Simeon boldly carried forth the Gospel for six years until he, too, was betrayed to the authorities by Justus -- the same man who cast his stone at

Constantine-Silvanus -- whereupon Simeon was apprehended and then burned at the stake in 690 CE.[398]

Accusations of Manichænism

To further quell the movement, the Catholic Church began making false accusations against the Paulicians' customs and beliefs, and deemed them to be heretics. The most damaging accusation was that they denied that Messiah took on an actual fleshly body; a tenet of *Manichæism*. The apostle John warns of denying the Son of God came in the flesh in 1 John 4:1-3. The Paulicians were mischaracterized as adhering to this heresy; an accusation the Catholic Church maintains to this day:

> "The Paulicians... rejected the Old Testament and parts of the New Testament, Baptism, the Eucharist, marriage, hierarchy, and cult, especially of the cross and pictures. They denied the reality of Christ's body and His Redemption..." (*Article, "Paulicians", McGraw-Hill, The Catholic University of America, 1967*)

While untrue the Paulicians rejected the "Old Testament," it is true they rejected baptismal regeneration, the sacrifice of the Mass, Transubstantiation, the sacrament of marriage as performed by a Catholic priest, and the Catholic priesthood

---

[398] *Decline and Fall of the Roman Empire*, Chap. 54

itself. They also adamantly opposed any form of image worship; a characteristic for which they were well-known.[399]

The Catholic Church twisted the Paulicians' adamant opposition to idolatry into a supposed proof that they rejected God-in-the-flesh. This was accomplished through the following rationale as set forth by John of Damascus:

- They [Paulicians] viewed adoration given physical objects or images as evil, despite their being called 'holy' or 'sacred.'

- By refusing to worship an image called 'Christ,' they rejected his Incarnation, the image being a visible testimony to his Incarnation.

- By rejecting his Incarnation, they rejected the true God.

This absurd reasoning was shared by leaders of the Second Council of Nicaea in 787 CE. Identification of the Paulicians with the *Manichæns* was specifically made at the Council's fifth session on October 4th. This Council also deemed the main purpose of representing Messiah by graven images was "that so the incarnation of the Word of God is shewn forth as real and not merely phantastic."[400] The term *'phantastic'* is derived from a Greek term meaning 'to appear.'

---

[399] E. B. Elliott, *Horæ Apocalypticæ*, vol. II, pp. 297-344, (London: 1862).
[400] Nicene and Post-Nicene Fathers, vol. 14, *The Seven Ecumenical Councils*, Edited by Schaff and Wace, (Mass.: Hendrickson Publishing, 1995), p. 550.

The accusation of *Manichænism* was a powerful political weapon which brought down upon the said heretic's head the full force of imperial legislation. Being labeled a *Manichænist* was tantamount to a death sentence. Other groups deemed heretical would lose rights of assembly or other civil rights, but seldom put to death. However, being a *Manichæns* was an offense for which the punishment was unalterably death.[401]

This fierce wave of persecution toward those holding to the New Covenant Passover and other apostolic institutions continued through the end of the eighth-century, and resulted in the deaths of an additional one hundred-thousand men, women, and children.[402]

> "During a period of one hundred and fifty years, these Christian churches seem to have been almost incessantly subjected to persecution, which they supported with Christian meekness and patience; as if the acts of their martyrdom, their preaching, and their lives were distinctly recorded, I see no reason to doubt that we should find in them the genuine successors of the Christians of the first two centuries."
> (*England: 1825; 5th Edition [Reformation History Library: Ages Digital Library, 1997]*)

---

[401] *The Paulician Heresy*, p. 196 (Paris: Mouton & Co.,1967).
[402] Constantine Porphyrog, *continuation* IV.16, p.103, Ed. Par.

The Key of Truth

British scholar and theologian Fred C. Conybeare made a remarkable literary discovery in the late nineteenth-century. Stored in an Armenian monastery were Paulician manuscripts dating back to the seventh- or eighth-century. Titled *The Key of Truth*, it contains many of the Paulicians' customs and beliefs:

- They believed a Christian is one who knows Christ, and keeps His commandments
- They believed the Church was a body of people; not a building
- They believed in the laying-on-of-hands for the "reception of the spirit"
- They baptized by full immersion
- They believed true repentance was a prerequisite for immersion
- They immersed only adults, citing Jesus' precedent of being 30 years of age
- They did not believe in the perpetual virginity of Mary
- They did not believe in adoration of the cross
- They rejected the Catholic mass, communion, and confession
- They were characterized by their obedience to the Ten Commandments
- They observed Passover and the Feast of Unleavened Bread, as well as the other Appointed Times.

"The [weekly] Sabbath was perhaps kept, and there were no special Sunday observances... Wednesday and Friday were not kept as fast days. Of the modern Christmas and of the Annunciation, and of the other feasts connected with the life of Jesus prior to his thirtieth year, this phase of the Church knew nothing. The general impression which the study leaves on us is that in it we have before us a form of church not very remote from the primitive Jewish Christianity of Palestine."
(Fred C. Conybeare, *Key of Truth,* page 193)

The Waldenses

Having again fled the region of persecution, many came to settle in a region between southern France and northern Italy. A stronghold resided in the valleys of the Piedmont there in northern Italy. The name *Vaudois* means "people of the valley," and became synonymous with this group of believers; although today they're more commonly known as *Waldenses*.

The name *Waldenses* may have derived from various origins. Some believe it stems from the name "Vaudois," while others believe it was adopted because of the group's twelfth-century leader, Peter Waldo.

Peter Waldo had been responsible for creating an early translation of the Scriptures into the *Romaunt* language (a combination of Middle English and Old French). This translation, in part, would become the Catholic Church's justification for banning Scripture from being read by layman.

In 1179 CE, disregarding the brutality of the Church from generations past, the Waldenses sent a delegation to Rome in order to attend the Third Council of the Lateran. They met with Pope Alexander III in hopes of persuading him to adopt some of their Biblical reforms. Instead, Pope Alexander III forbade them from preaching and prohibited them from offering any Scriptural interpretation without first obtaining authorization from their local clergy.

Undeterred, Waldo and the others developed an underground system whereby they traveled from town to town meeting secretly with likeminded believers. The traveling Waldensian preacher was known as a *barba,* and the group sheltered and housed him until arrangements were made for him to move on to the next town. As a result of this practice, the Waldenses were formally declared "schismatic" by Pope Lucius III in 1184 CE at the Synod of Verona.

The Waldenses strived to retain the doctrines emanated from Jesus and His apostles, believing that the truth had been corrupted after Emperor Constantine established Christianity as Rome's state-religion in the fourth-century.

"They declare themselves to be the apostles' successors, to have apostolical authority, and the keys of binding and loosing. They hold the Church of Rome to be the whore of Babylon, and

that all that obey her are damned, especially the clergy that have been subject to her since the time of pope Sylvester. They deny that any true miracles are wrought in the Church because none of themselves ever worked any. They hold that none of the ordinances of the Church, which have been introduced since Christ's ascension, ought to be observed, as being of no value. [Catholic] feasts, fasts, orders, blessings, offices of the church, and the like, they utterly reject..."
(William Jones, *The History of the Christian Church*, pp. 264-265)

"They despised all ecclesiastical customs which are not read in the gospel; such as Candlemas, Palm Sunday, the reconcilement of penitents, the adoration of the Cross on Good Friday, the feast of Easter, and the festivals of Christmas and the saints."
(C.H. Strong, *A Brief Sketch of the Waldenses*, p. 82-3)

"They observed the seventh day of the week according to the commandments, immersed for the believer's baptism, and kept the Passover ... once a year in the first month."
(*Persecutions and Atrocities on the Vaudois,* p. 348-349)

"Some of them hold that this sacrament Passover can only be celebrated by those that are good, others again by any that know the words of consecration..."
(William Jones, *The History of the Christian Church*, p. 265)

Yet upon the ascension of Pope Innocent III in 1198 CE, persecution intensified with new fury first towards the

Albigenses (another fundamentalist group in the valleys of France) and soon after the Waldenses. This same Pope declared, "Every cleric must obey the Pope, even if he commands what is evil; for no one may judge the Pope."

In 1211 CE, more than 80 Waldenses were burned to death at Strasbourg. In 1215 CE, the Waldenses were formally declared *heretics* at the Fourth Lateran Council which cited their principal error as "contempt for ecclesiastical power;" although it was also alleged their fundamentalist theology contained "innumerable errors."

Peter Waldo reputedly died in or around 1218 CE in Eastern Europe, possibly Germany, but he was never captured by papal powers and his ultimate demise remains unknown.

Some 300 years after Waldo, Pope Innocent VIII decided the "heresy" had gone on long enough. In 1487 CE, he issued a papal bull for the extermination of the Waldenses. Alberto de' Capitanei, archdeacon of Cremona, organized a crusade to carry out the bull. The extermination failed, but its inflicted brutality caused many of the Waldenses to flee to *Provence* and southern Italy where they endured another 200 years.

Then, in January of 1655 CE, the *Duke of Savoy* commanded all of the Waldenses in that region to either attend Catholic Mass or else move from the lower to the upper valleys. He allotted a mere twenty days for them to sell their lands and leave. Implemented in the middle of winter, the decree was intended to induce the Waldenses to compromise their faith in exchange for worldly comfort. Yet the majority of them, including old men and women as well as little children, "waded through the icy waters [and] climbed the frozen peaks" in order to worship God in the manner relayed in Scripture.

By mid-April, the Duke was aware his efforts to induce conformity had failed. Yet, tragically, he was unwilling to let the issue go. He devised a plan whereby he alleged false reports of Waldenses uprisings, and under that pretext sent troops into the upper valleys to quell the uprisings. The Duke demanded the local populace quarter his troops so as the troops had easy access to the populace. The Waldenses knew the uprisings were propaganda, and so gladly housed the troops in hopes of winning them over. But at 4:00 A.M. in the morning on April 24, 1655 CE, the signal was given to commence the massacre.

The Catholic forces didn't just slaughter the Waldenses, they unleashed a gruesome campaign of looting, rape, and torture. According to the account of Peter Liegé: "Little children were torn from the arms of their mothers, clasped by their tiny feet, and their heads dashed against the rocks; or were held between two soldiers and their quivering limbs torn up by main force. Their mangled bodies were then thrown on the highways or fields, to be devoured by beasts. The sick and the aged were burned alive in their dwellings. Some had their hands and arms and legs lopped off, and fire applied to the severed parts to staunch the bleeding and prolong their suffering. Some were flayed alive, some were roasted alive, some disemboweled; or tied to trees in their own orchards, and their hearts cut out. Some were horribly mutilated, and of others the brains were boiled and eaten by these cannibals. Some were fastened down into the furrows of their own fields, and ploughed into the soil as men plough manure into it. Others were buried alive. Fathers were marched to death with the heads of their sons suspended round their necks. Parents were compelled to look on while their children were first outraged [raped], then massacred, before being themselves permitted to die."

(James A. Wylie, *History of the Waldenses,* c1860)

An estimated 1700 Waldensians were barbarically slaughtered for no other reason than their uncompromising faith and commitment to worship God according to His commands. History records this massacre by the name, *The Piedmont Easter.*

John Milton (1608-1674), a famed Puritan writer best known for his script *Paradise Lost,* writes of the martyred Waldenses within his poem entitled, *On the Late Massacre in Piedmont*:

On the Late Massacre in Piedmont

Avenge, O Lord, thy slaughtered saints,
whose bones lie scattered on the Alpine mountains cold;
even them who kept thy truth so pure of old,
when all our fathers worshiped stocks and stones [idols]
Forget not: in thy book record their groans
Who were thy sheep, and in their ancient fold...

Summary

A remnant of God's people has always held to the *Feasts of the* LORD which include Passover, the Feast of Unleavened Bread, First-fruits, and others. Their stories are remarkable, and certainly not ones history should not have forgot. Heeding the warnings about false prophets and false doctrines, they recognized the apostate nature of this newer religious system and conversely strove to remain a community purified in accordance with Scriptural teachings. They opposed the ceremonies and worship of the dominant Church, they separated themselves from the world, and they refused to compromise God's Word even in the face of vicious persecution and bloodshed.

"For at least a thousand years before the Reformation the true church was composed of multitudes of simple Christians who were not part of the Roman system. That such believers existed, refused to be called 'Catholics,' and worshiped independently of the Roman hierarchy is history. It is a fact that they were pursued to imprisonment and death since at least the end of the fourth century."
(Dave Hunt, *A Woman Rides the Beast*, p. 254)

These commandment-keeping groups have been a thorn in the flesh of the Papacy since its inception. They've stood as a perpetual witness against Rome, and in so doing have exposed her as an apostate, blood drunken harlot who has perverted the Gospel and exalted a mere man (the Pope) to the level of God upon earth.

The Quartodecimans, Paulicians, Waldenese and others did not consider Good Friday – Easter Sunday to be an appropriate holiday even though it had been "Christianized," and even though God "knew in their hearts" they weren't worshipping the pagan deities from which Easter originated.

It goes without saying that keeping the *Feasts of the LORD* was not the only practice which incited the Catholic Church to persecute them; but having chose to disobey the modern equivalent of Pharisees who rules allegedly supersede the commandments of God, these vigilant brethren suffered wrath and defamation of character enduring to this very day.

"It is now clearly known that the Paulicans were not Manicheans … The Albigenses [too] were oppressed on account of this sentiment, which accusation was also made against the Waldenses. Care must be taken on this point, and too prompt credence should not be given to the accuser. The Roman Catholic Church sought diligently for excuses to persecute. Even Luther was declared by the Synod of Sens to be a Manichean." (Acland, *The Glorious Recovery of the Vadois*, 1xvii, London, 1857)

History is always written by the winners. Thus far, the god of this world has put forth disinformation about those who've faithfully kept the *Feasts of the LORD* throughout the Church age. However, the back of the Good Book foretells the liar's time is about to end. The sealed *scroll of Title* has been purchased by the God of Abraham, Isaac, and Jacob. When He takes possession, the truth in all matters shall be revealed!

For more documentation of Messiah's
fulfillment of the *Sign of Jonah,*
be sure to get the follow-up book:

Messiah's Final 50 Days:
An Alternate Chronology in Light of the Sign of Jonah

www.sign-of-jonah.com

Made in the USA
Charleston, SC
02 October 2014